THE BOOK OF THE
ZODIAC

THE BOOK OF THE
ZODIAC

An historical anthology of astrology

BY FRED GETTINGS

Ward Lock Ltd, London

For Sandy, with her Moon in Taurus

ISBN: 0 7063 1357 7
Published by Ward Lock Ltd, London, England
Produced by Trewin Copplestone Publishing Ltd
Copyright 1972 © Fred Gettings
Reproduction by City Engraving Co. (Hull) Ltd.
Printed in Great Britain by Sir Joseph Causton
& Sons Ltd, London and Eastleigh.

CONTENTS

The number references at the end of each quotation indicate the date of publication, and the reference to the bibliography on page 139 ff. The references after certain captions will be found explained on page 139.

1. *Man standing in the zodiacal womb, his sexual energies at the still point of the turning cosmos. Not only is he contained within the cosmos, but he also contains a cosmos within himself, the one a reflection of the other. This is the one graphic version of the esoteric meaning behind astrology, the more profound statement underlying the popular version opposite. (From Fludd).*

2. *The popular zodiacal man. Each of the 12 signs has a rulership over a different part of the body. Aries rules the head, which is why the Ram is lying on the man's head. This is a popular statement of the relationship between stars and man.*

1

INTRODUCTION

Tell someone that you're interested in astrology, and nine times out of ten the reaction will be a raised eyebrow, perhaps an amused smile and a look implying that with all this star gazing, your head is stuck in the clouds. But at the same time, the contradictions of human nature being what they are, that person will almost in the same breath give you his date of birth, and from this expect you to produce an instant character reading, along with a blow by blow account of his life for the next forty years!

Confused by potted predictions in the 'astrology' columns of popular newspapers and magazines — which have in fact *nothing* to do with serious astrology — few people have any real idea of what this ancient art is all about. Nowadays there is an increasing and genuine, deep desire to understand just why, for thousands of years, it has been believed by so many intelligent people that the planets in our solar system should appear to have an effect on people born on the earth. People are indeed beginning to ask once more about the truth behind astrology, and some are beginning to realize that astrology represents the most complete psychological system which has survived from the past. Indeed, many now realize that astrology is a tool by which it may be possible to understand life, as well as people — and is particularly adapted as a means for studying the self. It is not too much to claim that astrology is rooted in a mystery within which may be found the key to the majority of the problems facing the human race today. As one seventeenth-century astrologer sums up astrology:

...for therein is consulted the whole progress of

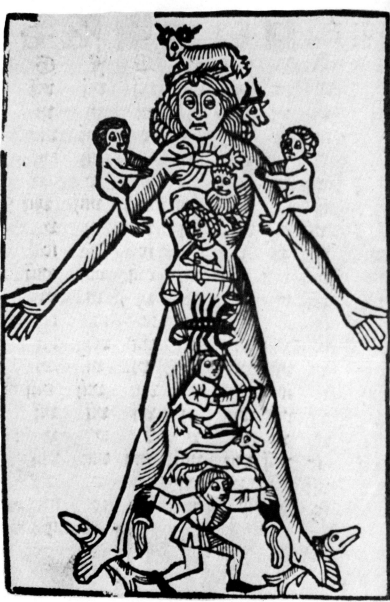

3. *The modern horoscope of Oliver Cromwell.*

4. *A simplified version of Cromwell's horoscope, showing the influence of Aries and Taurus.*

5. *An eighteenth century version of Cromwell's horoscope (From* Sibly).

6. *Mars and his rulerships. One notes the violence associated with this God: Mars has rulership over war, but he may also bring about needed reforms.*

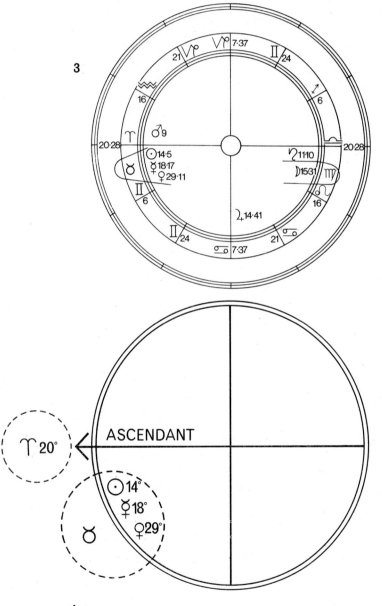

Man, from his Birth to his Burial; and by that alone we are enabled to discover the times of his happy and inauspicious Fortunes. (1679:1) Thus does John Gadbury begin one hundred choice aphorisms on the nature of astrology. It is perhaps relevant that the last of the aphorisms sets out a social situation in regard to astrology which is unfortunately true to this day:

The art of Astrology is certain and most indubitably true, but there are few that Practise it, who rightly understand it. (1679:2) The following twelve chapters present an introduction to the theory of the twelve types and their associations, but in order to understand the material properly, it is essential that we first of all clarify certain ideas. Everyone knows that the twelve signs of the zodiac each present different characteristics, and most people are aware of the major characteristics attached to their own sign: usually indeed they are aware of the faults, if not the virtues, of the sign under which their partner was born! This attitude to astrology is partly right, and partly wrong. No good astrologer will pretend that the whole of humanity can be slotted precisely into twelve clearly defined types: but most will agree that each individual has one of the signs emphasised at the moment of birth and may therefore be considered a 'native' of that sign. The Sun moves through the twelve signs during the course of the year, and popular belief holds that a person's zodiacal Sign is that in which the Sun appears to be at the time of birth. For example, because the Sun is in Aries between approximately 21st March and 20th April, most people born during that time assume that they were 'born under Aries'. The Sun is indeed an important factor, since it rules the conscious aim of a person, but it is by no means the only or the most important clue to the predominant sign governing the individual. Astrologers usually take the Ascendant as being the most important and influential single point in the horoscope. The Ascendant is that part of the zodiac which is arising over the horizon at the moment of birth, and when astrologers talk of a person being 'born under a particular sign' they usually have this Ascendant in mind. Thus while one might think that Oliver Cromwell (figure 3) was Taurean (because he was born at a time when the Sun was in the sign Taurus), most astrologers would consider him to be of the Aries type, because the Ascendant is in Aries (figure 4). This is an important point, because it means that one is not always of the zodiacal type the popular form of astrology would have one believe. The Ascendant is not *always* the most important point, the determinant of the 'type': when several plantets are found together in one sign the qualities of that sign will be emphasised in the horoscope. Thus, if we look at Cromwell's horoscope again, we see that besides being strongly Aries he is also very strongly Taurean, because he has three planets in Taurus (figure 4). The Moon is a strong force in a horoscope, and very often the Sign occupied by the Moon shows its influence in a personality. Thus we see that the Ascendant, the Sun, the Moon and the planets all contribute to the general character of people, and one is on dubious grounds when one insists that any individual is purely of one type, 'born under one sign'.

It is very rare for anyone to be born with the Sun, the Ascendant, several planets and the Moon all in one sign, and therefore we must conclude that nearly everyone is a mixture of several different signs, and the product of the harmonies and tensions engendered by these different signs. However, there is no doubt that one sign tends to predominate in every personality, and any astrologer worth his salt can usually, almost at a glance, determine which sign is strongest merely from a person's appearance. Having determined the predominating sign in this way the astrologer is usually able to draw conclusions concerning the personality, temperament, virtues and vices of the native. This is one reason why it is useful to learn something of the physical attributes and the accompanying characteristics of the twelve Signs — it enables one to be choosy or sensible about one's relationships, for example, and to understand something of the world of people from a study of their outer appearance.

Each of the signs is ruled by a particular planet, Aries for example is ruled by Mars, Taurus by Venus. The characteristics of these

5

6

planets are themselves partly responsible for the qualities manifested by the signs: for example the masculine and aggressive planet Mars makes many Aries types masculine and aggressive. A planet may manifest in two ways — either it may work freely, or as they would say in the past, in a 'dignified manner'; or it may work in a restricted way, in an 'ill-dignified' manner. Because of this, each sign may also manifest itself in either a 'good' or a 'bad' way depending on whether or not the Sign, or the planet ruling it, is under pressure. The traditional account of the way such 'dual' influences work may be seen, for example, with Mars on page 22, Venus on page 40. The fact that there are only seven planets listed in early accounts brings us to the point that in modern times three recently discovered planets, Uranus, Neptune and Pluto, have been incorporated into the astrological system. Uranus has taken over from Saturn in its rule over Aquarius, Neptune has taken over from Jupiter in its rule of Pisces, and Pluto has taken over from Mars in its rule of Scorpio. Thus, to a certain extent, astrologers have had to remodel slightly the astrological doctrine following the discovery of new planets, and this partly accounts for some of the changes which have taken place in astrological teachings during the past hundred years or so. Most modern astrologers now accept the following rulerships of the planets over the signs:

Aries — ruled by Mars.
Taurus — ruled by Venus.
Gemini — ruled by Mercury.
Cancer — ruled by the Moon.
Leo — ruled by the Sun.
Virgo — ruled by Mercury.
Libra — ruled by Venus.
Scorpio — ruled by Pluto, formerly by Mars.
Sagittarius — ruled by Jupiter.
Capricorn — ruled by Saturn.
Aquarius — ruled by Uranus, formerly by Saturn.
Pisces — ruled by Neptune, formerly by Jupiter.

The many rich associations for the Signs and planets are based on the old doctrine of

ARIES
21 March to
20 April
Planet: Mars ♂
Glyph: ♈
Keynote: Hope
Watchword:
Variety

TAURUS
21 April to
20 May
Planet: Venus ♀
Glyph: ♉
Keynote: Peace
Watchword:
Stability

GEMINI
21 May to 21 June
Planet: Mercury ☿
Glyph: ♊
Keynote: Joy
Watchword:
Variety

CANCER
22 June to 22 July
Planet: Moon ☽
Glyph: ♋
Keynote:
Patience
Watchword:
Sympathy

* *These dates refer to the approximate period during which the Sun is in the sign. The dates sometimes vary by a day or so in each year.*

LEO
23 July to
22 August
Planet: Sun ☉
Glyph: ♌
Keynote: Glory
Watchword:
Faith

SAGITTARIUS
23 November to
23 December
Planet: Jupiter ♃
Glyph: ♐
Keynote:
Wisdom
Watchword:
Liberty

VIRGO
23 August to
22 September
Planet: Mercury ☿
Glyph: ♍
Keynote: Purity
Watchword:
Service

CAPRICORN
23 December to
20 January
Planet: Saturn ♄
Glyph: ♑
Keynote:
Reverence
Watchword:
Ambition

LIBRA
23 September to
22 October
Planet: Venus ♀
Glyph: ♎
Keynote: Beauty
Watchword:
Harmony

AQUARIUS
21 January to
19 February
Planet: Uranus ♅
Glyph: ♒
Keynote: Truth
Watchword:
Research

SCORPIO
23 October to
22 November
Planet: Pluto ♇
Glyph: ♏
Keynote: Justice
Watchword:
Power

PISCES
20 February to
20 March
Planet: Neptune ♆
Glyph: ♓
Keynote: Love
Watchword:
Sensitivity

7

7. *Sagittarius, from a medieval manuscript. (British Museum).*

8. *The doctrine of signatures: it could be that the unicorn is linked with Sagittarius because the horn is rather like the arrow of Sagittarius, which is potentially dangerous but rarely used by the native for harmful purposes: the unicorn, like Sagittarius, is of a gentle nature, in spite of its power. From De la Porte.*

8

signatures, the idea being that physical resemblances in themselves imply spiritual resemblances (figure 8), and that the links perceived on the material level of the world indicate a link on a higher, invisible level. The associations, therefore, are often useful in presenting the inner nature of a particular sign: for example, there is a quaint relevance in saying that Sagittarius resembles a unicorn, Gemini a monkey, and the Scorpionic a water snake. Anyone who can grasp the inner quality of these creatures is already well on the way to grasping the inner nature of the signs with which they are associated.

In spite of the rich associations and doctrines which have survived from the past concerning the twelve zodiacal types, the traditional characteristics of the twelve signs have not always been the same throughout history. For example, Cancer and Pisces — both governed by 'changeable' planets — have changed their personalities considerably over two thousand years. Some signs, notably Sagittarius, have retained their general characteristics remarkably well, whilst others, such as Scorpio and Capricorn, have gained reputations they scarcely deserved. Because of this, it is fascinating to look at the different traditions concerning the twelve signs through the words of the astrologers who have contributed to the traditional lore. Not only is it interesting to study how one's own Sign has changed, to study the various ramifications of the teaching in regard to oneself — it is also useful and interesting to see how remarkably apposite the traditions are in regard to the people one knows in ordinary life. Some of the traditions are merely amusing, but all are informative in one way or another, and all of value to anyone interested in the Self.

A seventeenth-century list of significations attached to the twelve zodiacal signs sets the general theme:

Aries incites a man or person to be witty, ingenious.

Taurus makes one more laborious.

Gemini represents one witty, deceitful, and yet a lover of Arts and Learning.

Cancer an unconstant variable creature, never fixt.

Leo, a grave, sober, discreet person, whether man or woman.

Virgo, one loving Learning and Arts, coveteous, cruel or despightful, well-willer to War.

Libra, one inconstant, crafty, a contemner of all Arts, conceited of his own person.

Scorpio, an impudent fellow, a brazen face, yet of good understanding, coveteous, arrogant.

Sagittarius, shews one Valiant, and without fear.

Capricorn, portends a letcherous person, much given to the flesh, nor constant to his Wife or Mistress.

Aquarius, Intimates a very humane affable party. Speaking soberly, envious to none; constant to his opinion.

Pisces, argues a stammering person, fradulent, and a pretender to the Truth. (1671:*3*)

This from a textbook by one William Thrasher who appears with some signs to be living up to his name! The quotations show how, even in the seventeenth century, many of the types were misunderstood. Who would recognise himself here? Leo is scarcely sober or discreet

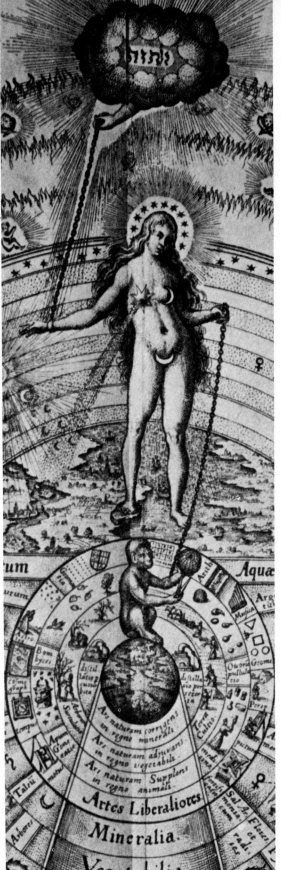

9

9. *The spirit of man caught between heaven and the earth. Anima Mundi is chained alike to heaven and hell — man must either evolve, refine his spirit to become more godlike, or sink lower, and become more bestial.* (*from* Fludd).

10. *The zodiacal woman.* (*from* Sibly).

nowadays; Capricorn is not *merely* lecherous, one would hope; Pisces is an altogether different person from the one which Thrasher presents. Yet Thrasher was a serious astrologer, who himself expressed regret at the way astrologers were inclined to present their material badly and inaccurately. Things have changed, quite clearly. Why bother to look into such material, as traditional astrology, much of which is so obviously a tangled mess? Perhaps we are interested in the truth; or even interested in the unravelling of the truth, which has a beauty of its own. The interest is worth-while, for behind this tattered tradition, behind all the complexities and differences of modern teaching, there lies a doctrine which is clear and useful — so useful, indeed, that it was claimed:

One skilful in this science may evade many effects of the stars, when he knows their natures, and diligently prepares himself to receive their effects.

(2nd century A.D. — *4*).

Astrology is not concerned merely with learning to control one's destiny, it is connected also with the idea of self-knowledge, and there are few things more certain to reveal one's own prejudices than a serious attempt to study astrology. The Reverend John Butler, of Lichfield, wished to depose astrology and thus weaken its influence in England, and so he studied the subject deeply — more deeply than most who attempt to depose it, or even merely hold opinions about it. The result was the growth of a reverence for this great art, and finally he could admit:

Next to Theology, nothing leads me more nearer to the sight of God than the sacred astrological study of the great works of Nature.

16

11

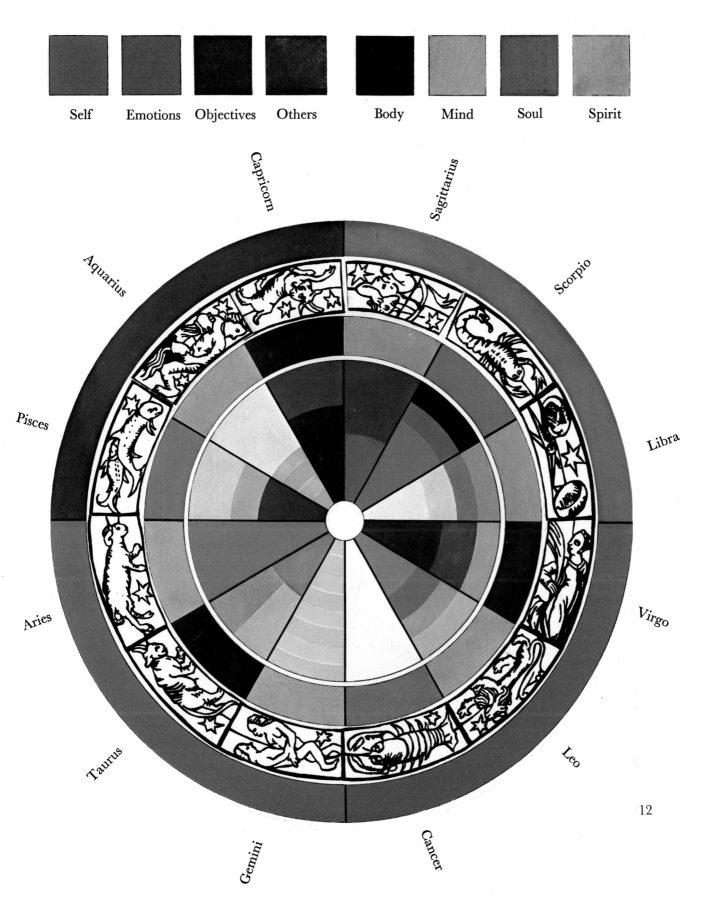

Self Emotions Objectives Others Body Mind Soul Spirit

13. *Aries in the fixed stars (from Bevis).*
14. *Aries, from fifteenth century book on astrology. The Ram does not look at all belligerent.*
15. *The Aries type, as an assertive, militant leader.*
16. *Mars in his chariot of war. Impetuous, assertive and brash, like the Aries types he rules.*

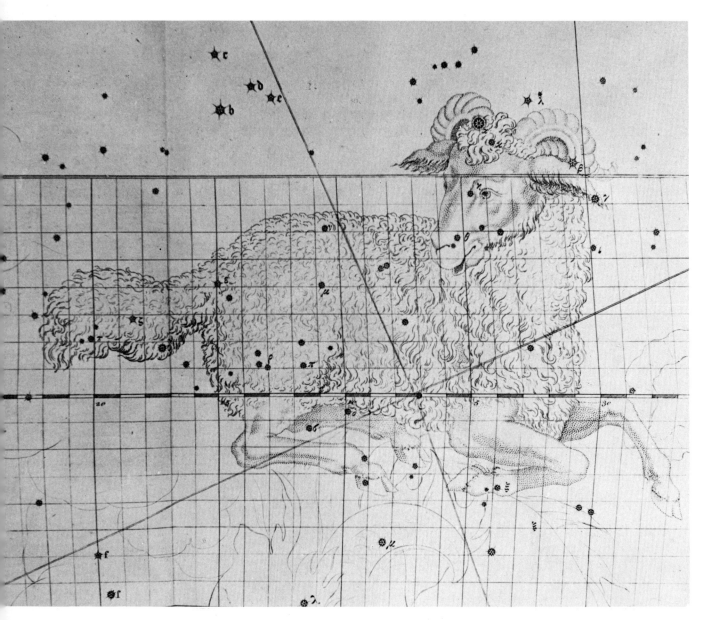

13

ARIES

14

The Sun in Aries describes usually one of good stature, strong, and well-made; a good complexion, yellowish, flaxen, or sandy hair; courageous, and martially disposed; likely to succeed in the army or in the medical profession, fortunate; and victorious over his enemies. (1879:*1*)

Already it seems that we note a contradiction, for our type will succeed in the army, where the aim is destruction, as well as in the medical profession, where the aim is healing, but perhaps the contradiction is resolved when we realize that Aries rules over cutting instruments and thus over bayonets, as well as over scalpels. Arietans will leap forward regardless, being always the first to attack, yet we fail to understand the type if we do not realize that they really do care for people. Aries, for all its aggressiveness, likes people — the nature of this pugnacious type is, therefore, surprisingly constructive, for it is essentially enthusiastic. Arietans will throw themselves wholeheartedly into whatever they set out to do: be it the act of destroying or the act of healing or regenerating. The astrological tradition has on the whole been unfair to Aries, for it has tended in one period to concentrate on one side of the nature, and at another period on the other side: at one time the bayonet is admired, at another time the scalpel. The early descriptions of our type are unfair, as they generally portray the more lurid and violent side of life to which this unrestrained Arietan enthusiasm may be dedicated. This we see even in an eighteenth-century image:

Aries...usually contributes unto the native a dry body, lean and spare, strong and large bones and limbs, piercing eyes, a swarthy or

15

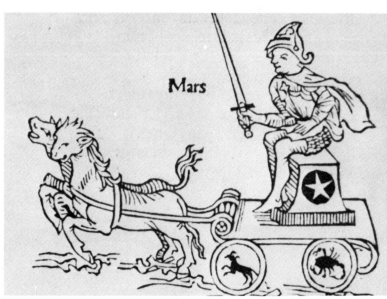

Mars

16

18

17

19

sallow complexion, and sandy-coloured or red hair, and inclines him to be choleric, brutal, violent, and intemperate... (1795:2)

Certainly not fair on Aries, and perhaps what is more to the point, scarcely a description of a ram! Is Aries a ram at all, we might well ask, when we view the rather unpleasant image of a 'brutal, violent, and intemperate' type? Astrologers have insisted on the connection, suggesting that the glyph for the sign is a drawing of a ram's horns, which they patently are not, and even by suggesting that the type is something of a 'battering ram' in the way it goes about life, constantly pioneering and championing causes, even lost causes. But the connection with the ram is slight, on historical as well as psychological grounds, for the ram will only butt people when its own area is trespassed upon, while most Arietans will cheerfully butt people without a reason, out of sheer high spirits and a sense of competition! Not surprisingly, therefore, Aries has rulership over all the warlike and strong countries — or at least over countries which were warlike, strong and pioneering in other centuries — including England, France and Germany — and we constantly find that images of Aries insist upon the violence and impetuosity of the type, taking us further and further away from the relatively peaceful ram. It is evident, therefore, that we should not look towards the ram in our attempt to understand Aries — we must in fact look towards Mars, the powerful Roman god of war who rules over the sign. Mars controls such things as 'thunder and lightning, fiery meteors, pestilential air, and all strange phenomena in the heavens', and his aggressive nature is seen in the animals, in the herbs and plants, and even in the diseases over which he has dominion:

The mastiff, wolf, tiger, cockatrice, panther, and all such beasts as are ravenous and wild... all stinging water serpents and voracious fish. Wormwood, monks-hood, leeks... devil's milk, nettles, ginger, pepper... and all trees that are prickly and thorny.

Pestilential fevers, plagues...burnings and scaldings...all choleric diseases, wounds or bruises by iron...and all effects proceeding

17. *Aries, from fifteenth century manuscript. (British Museum)*
18. *Mars the war-lord, governing Aries.*
19. *Painting by the Aries artist Goya, 'Street Fighting on the 2nd May, 1808' (Madrid). The colours and subject are typical Arietan.*
20. *Portrait of a soldier. The red jacket in favour up to the end of the nineteenth century, is typical of Aries.*

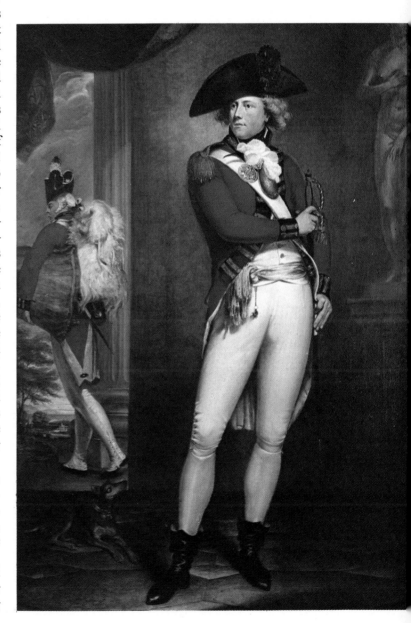

21

from intemperate anger and passion...(1795:*3*) This is the stuff Arietans are made of, and it is not surprising that with such associations as these the traditional image of Aries should be coloured a little with blood and thunder, for all persons born under Aries are by definition born under the dominion of Mars. According to our eighteenth-century astrologer, the person born under the sway of Mars:

> will inherit a courageous and invincible disposition: unsusceptible of fear or danger; hazarding his life on all occasions, and in all perils; subject to no reason in war or contention; unwilling to obey or submit to any superior; regardless of all things in comparison of triumphing over his enemy or antagonist; and yet prudent in the management and direction of his private concerns. (1795:*4*)

As if this image of a type represented a 'socially acceptable' human being, the same astrologer goes on to draw a darker picture, of the type under the sway of an 'afflicted or ill dignified' Mars:

> the party will then grow up a trumpeter of his own fame and consequence, without decency or honesty; a lover of malicious quarrels and affrays; prone to wickedness and slaughter, and in danger of committing murder, of robbing on the highway, of becoming a thief, traitor, or incendiary; of a turbulent spirit, obscene, rash, inhuman and treacherous, fearing neither God nor man, given up to every species of fraud, violence, cruelty, and oppression. (1795:*5*)

The stage villain incarnate, and those with a sense of humour may hiss! Sensitive Arietan souls, who may be tempted to close this book for very shame, must leap a century to a time when martial qualities were better valued, and note a more generous presentation of the virtuous Aries:

> He is the Captain, the Leader, Pioneer among men; going out in sympathy to a new thought, rapidly assimilating fresh ideas, always in the van of progress in whatever kind of work — intellectual, artistic or practical — he may take up. He gets close quarters in his battles, and when highly developed, fights best with his head; that is to say, in the field of thought

... They really enjoy facing and overcoming difficulties, and will go out of their way to challenge opposition rather than forego the exercise of their faculties. Hope and enthusiasm are with them wherever they go and their happy knack of forgetting failure helps them through times of stress and strain and anxiety that would break down the courage of any other type... Enthusiastic friendship fills a large place in the emotional life...no type is warmer-hearted, or more frank and generous in showing affection; but, even among the highly developed, these tendencies are apt to lead to trouble, and the sorrows that follow upon rash engagements and imprudent marriages are among the forms of discipline that they are called upon to face... If falling in love is, even for the highly developed specimens, a dangerously headlong performance, falling out of love is, at the primitive stage, more dangerously headlong still, for loyalty and tenacity are not among the virtues of this sign, and the desire for change of surrounding and companionship is difficult to master. (1911:*6*)

It seems that we have meandered willy-nilly back to at least one definite attribute of the ram — the sexuality associated with the type. Sex is a big thing with Aries, and so it is not surprising that the sign for Mars is still used by biologists to represent the male principle. Aries loves the chase, and is not averse to chasing more than one quarry at a time. The chase over, the victory won, the Arietan only too often simply goes away. No wonder that he has something of a bad reputation as far as his love affairs are concerned, and perhaps this alone helps to account for the persistence of the 'ram' image.

Merely because the peculiar limitations of our English language keep us referring to 'him' and to 'his', we must not think that these words do not apply to the female of the species: the female Arietan is just as intense in the chase, just as exaggerated, just as romantic, just as inconstant, and ultimately just as independent.

And so we see that Aries does have many virtues and strengths, but the unfortunate thing is that the stage villain catches the attention of

21. *The bramble. Aries rules sharp, stinging plants, and dangerous ones — monks-hood, garlic, mustard, onion, and the like.*
22. *The plague in Italy. Mars rules sudden and unexpected death, as well as the plague.*
23. *The burning of Savonarola in Florence. Aries rules large fires, executions, and Florence. Savonarola was himself an Aries type.*

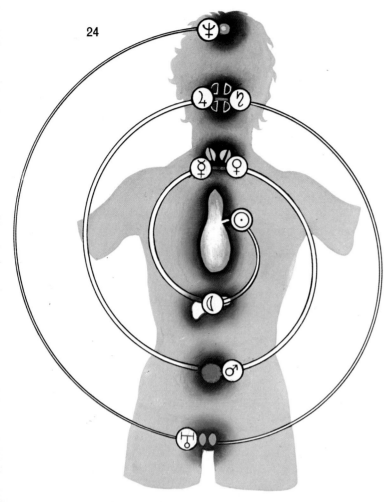

24

24. *An up-to-date version of the planetary rulerships in the human body. The Sun rules the thymus gland, the Moon the pancreas, Mercury the thyroid, Venus the parathyroid, Mars the solar-plexus, Jupiter the post pituitary, Saturn the anterior, Uranus rules the sex glands, Neptune that strange pineal gland, popularly called 'the third eye'. The glandular secretions predominate at different*

people more easily than does the energetic angel. When the seventeenth-century astrologer Gadbury decided to record a hundred worthy sayings about astrology, in writing of Mars, a planet which may be constructive, energetic, and the great injector of courage, he chose the blood and thunder image instead:

Mars...makes notorious lyars and Inventors of Fables, and great contrivers of mischief, perjur'd, turbulent and evil-minded men. (1679:7)

Partly true, all this, but only partly. Aries is not always strictly honest in speech — and by this we must not take it that they are always 'notorious Lyars', but that their natural tendency to exaggeration and their strong imagination often unite in such a way as to distort the truth. Many Arietans often believe the lie they tell and may become quite indignant, quite 'martially disposed', if openly accused of lying. Better give the Arietan the benefit of the doubt, and assume not a dishonest heart or tongue, but an over-fertile imagination, for if you do this you think of him not as an evil man, but as an artist, and surely no artist can be entirely evil.

Arietans go to extremes in all things, and this in virtues as much as in vices. To be fair to Aries, then, we may dismiss their lower nature and concentrate our attention on the many things in which they are excellent, noting that while Aries is not a dual sign, it does tend to go to extremes, so that there is a *good* Arietan, and a *bad* Arietan, and little in between:

The first are the pioneering and reforming leaders of men; frank, candid, intense, intellectual, aspiring; perhaps a little too 'touchy', assertive, exaggerative, and venturesome. The second place self-interest above principle, are aggressive, presumptuous, too changeable, inconstant, and sensitive, yet inconsiderate of others; magnifying everything that engages their attention, as well as their own powers. They ape their superiors, ever seeking to place themselves on an equality with them, are unduly familiar and personal, and if one gives them the proverbial 'inch' they promptly take a 'yard'. These personal Arians are typical usurpers. (1917:8)

periods of physical growth, in a sequence indicated by the spiral. It is suggested that Pluto has rule over some function as yet unrecognized in man.

25. *The city of Florence, ruled by Aries. (workshop of Francesco Rosselli?)*

26. *The four 'humours', or 'temperaments', linked with excesses and deficiencies in the astrological elements in man.*

27

The 'personal Arians' are those who *abuse* the qualities of the sign. Let us forget about them, and pay attention to those who *use* the qualities of the sign constructively.

Aries gives character almost larger than life, and one which would appeal to the Victorians who, for all their alleged stuffiness, produced individuals who pioneered an empire through the Arietan disposition to 'make discoveries, and become noted for his explorations'. People who will go to extremes, do or die, are valuable when an empire is being built, and perhaps this is why the Arietans were so popular in the nineteenth century, why Aries had a good write-up in the astrological text books, why accounts of his strengths and virtues were given with a sense of respect, as is rarely the case nowadays!

Aries...renders the person born under its influence straight-forward, ingenious, frank, disposed to leadership and command, enterprising and industrious, courting difficulties with a view to conquest, generous, even to extravagance, determined, aspiring, active, manly, enthusiastic in religion and politics, subtle, combative, and often bigoted, though generally speaking, progressive in his tendencies; liable to change his views and object, but at all times enthusiastic in the pursuit of a prevailing idea. His tastes are disposed to be fastidious in many things. The native will desire to shine, to gain honours and prominence, but will have difficulties, equal only to his own courage and determination... The powers of the Aries person are more versatile than profound, and he is more successful in executive mental work, more capable of command than organization; often a strong reformer, but more destructive of existing orders than constructive of new ones. The temper is quick, vivacious, fretful and capricious. Eloquence of a declamatory, and sometimes a violent kind, is given by this sign. Where there is much smoke the fire burns long, but here it is all flame, and the anger of the Aries man is a thing of the hour only. Quick to anger, but soon pacified, the native does not bear long resentment. The destiny will be changeful. Not infrequently, the native possesses estate in the country, and has an aptitude for farming... He gains wealth by marriage, but will have difficulties through females in connection with his monetary affairs, maybe a legal suit. In the pursuit of industries he is successful. He is likely to be an only son, or to become such from the demise of a younger brother. In early life he will have difficulties in connection with his business, and disputes in the family, and if the Sun be below the Earth, he will lose his father early. Journeys will be caused by family matters, or by reason of disputes and enmities. He will be disposed to ballooning or climbing of high mountains... In the married state there will be strife and danger of divorce or separation. The sign gives few or no children, but should any live they will rise to good position and receive honours. The native is likely to marry early, and there is likely to be disaffection and inconstancy as a consequence... (1893:9)

In all, if one brings the passages up to date, by changing the 'ballooning' to some other active and potentially dangerous sport, and by cutting down the chance of infant mortality, we are left with an excellent description of the modern Arietan, though it must be understood that nowadays the chance of an Arietan escaping with less than one marriage is even less likely than before.

Aries has a reputation for being self-destructive, of being accident prone: 'The native, by excess of rashness, will be liable to a short life and violent death' is an example from the previous author, though here once more we are verging on blood and thunder. Looking at the reputation in a sensible way, however, we do see the major problem which confronts every Arietan as being one of self-control — not merely because rashness may lead to predicament, for rashness may also be useful, but because the purpose of the Arietan life is to learn something about emotional control. Those Arietans who are not 'highly evolved' are rather young, in the sense of being perhaps brash or inexperienced, and the purpose of their life is to grow up emotionally, which is of course connected with the idea of self-control. Alan Leo had much to say about the need for the

27. *Self-portrait with a bandaged ear, by Van Gogh. The self-mutilation and suicide of Van Gogh, who had Aries strongly marked in his chart (below), are prefigured in his horoscope. His Sun and Mercury are in Aries, his Ascendant Cancer, on the fixed star Pollux. (See pages 58 and 59).*

28. *Portrait of an Aries type. (from Varley).*

Aries.

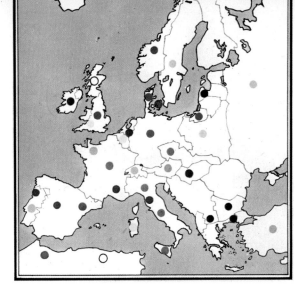

29. *Certain traditional sign rulerships over parts of Europe. The key below the world map also applies to this plate. England is ruled by Aries, Ireland by Taurus, Scotland by Cancer, and (very probably) Wales by Capricorn, though some astrologers suggest Gemini for this country.*

🔴 ARIES		🔵 LIBRA	
🟤 TAURUS		⚫ SCORPIO	
🟡 GEMINI		⚫ SAGITTARIUS	
⚪ CANCER		⚫ CAPRICORN	
🔴 LEO		🟡 AQUARIUS	
🟡 VIRGO		🟡 PISCES	

30. *Certain traditional sign rulerships over parts of the world. The U.S.A. is traditionally under Cancer, but Gemini is much more likely.*

31. *Italy is ruled by the creative Leo, as would befit the cradle of the Renaissance.*

32. *Cyprus is ruled by Venus, and it is traditionally in Cyprus (at Paphos) that Venus was supposed to have been born.*

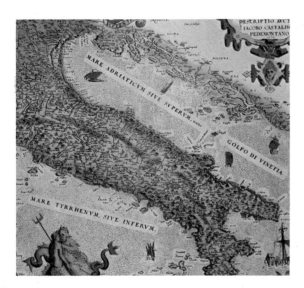

31

32

30

33

34

35

36

33. *An aspiring and gentle Aries, striving upwards.*
34. *Etching by the Arietan artist Goya (from 'The Disasters of War').*
35. *The lower Aries nature. Aries rules the wolf and many other dangerous animals.*

36. *The glyph for Mars, when in its rightful position, points up to heaven, the cross of matter lifted by the circle of spirit. When under pressure, it may point downwards, to hell! The picture represents the great 'chain of being' which links all sentient creatures, along which all must ascend or descend, between Heaven and Hell.*

Mars influence to be controlled:

In every nativity Mars shows the courage, capacity for heroism, endurance, strength and power: thus Mars can work for good as well as for evil: and, indeed, it is only when its influence is perverted, when the force given by this planet is abused, that it 'mars' the fortunes and leads the native to destruction. (1904:*10*)

The moral is that if the Arietan can practise a certain degree of self control, then his life will go relatively well, and (what is more important) the purpose of his life will be achieved.

In the unregenerate and lower and less evolved types of humanity the martial influence arouses the desire to annihilate or destroy foes and enemies, which desire when knowledge is gained changes to an attitude of defensiveness and alertness. Circumstances and environment call out all those active, outrushing impulses which eventually cause men to be acute, keen and sharp-witted; so that from sheer muscular strength and a state in which boldness, defiance, temerity and hardihood, or even foolhardiness, is the main expression of the life, we find fortitude, courage and strength, enabling the native, through practice and experience, to attain to 'skill in action'... In the undeveloped man who has not learned to control his passions the bestial and brutal, or sensual desires, run riot until the slowly growing MIND begins to take the upper hand. Then in the mental world Mars gradually loses its power over man; for there a higher and more subtle force is waiting to humanise the man and gradually wean him from the plane of the senses. But so long as the senses, governed by Mars, dominate the mind, then the mind itself is coarsened and made tricky and designing.

In the physical world Mars causes accidents, fevers and violence. But if we could see the growth of the Ego, if we could trace its history, we should find that impulses and rash action in the past had brought its inevitable reaction in accident or fever; for every effort has its cause, and there are no mishaps or misadventures which could not be traced to a cause set in motion by the Ego in the past... On the physical plane most of the adverse influence of Mars is, as it were, a 'ready-money transaction'. Men who rise to positions far above the sphere of their birth used the influence of Mars in what we call 'grit' — strength of character, be that character good or bad... At the present day, the influence of Mars is mostly seen in self-assertion and in a struggle to maintain self-interests. But in those who are developed, the true Martians, we find the power to direct, to govern, to superintend: they have courage and confidence in their ability to accomplish and achieve the ends sought for. (1904:*11*)

Here we have it on the line, as straight as any Arietan could wish: the purpose of the Arietan life is involved with self-control. The Arietan is a kind of receiving station: he receives vibrations from Mars, vibrations which are relatively coarse, and these he must learn to transmit refined. This is why an Arietan of high evolution, one who has struggled with the selfhood which identification with animal passions implies, is a very remarkable man indeed, one with the outer form of a man and the inner spirit of a god.

37

37. *Titian, Venus of Urbino (Uffizi).
The luxury-loving, matrialistic
Taurus is governed by the sensuous
Venus.*

38. *'Still Life' by the Taurean painter
Delacroix (Louvre). The Taurean
love of good food was hinted at in
this picture. That which Aries will
shoot or slaughter, Taurus will
gladly eat!*

38

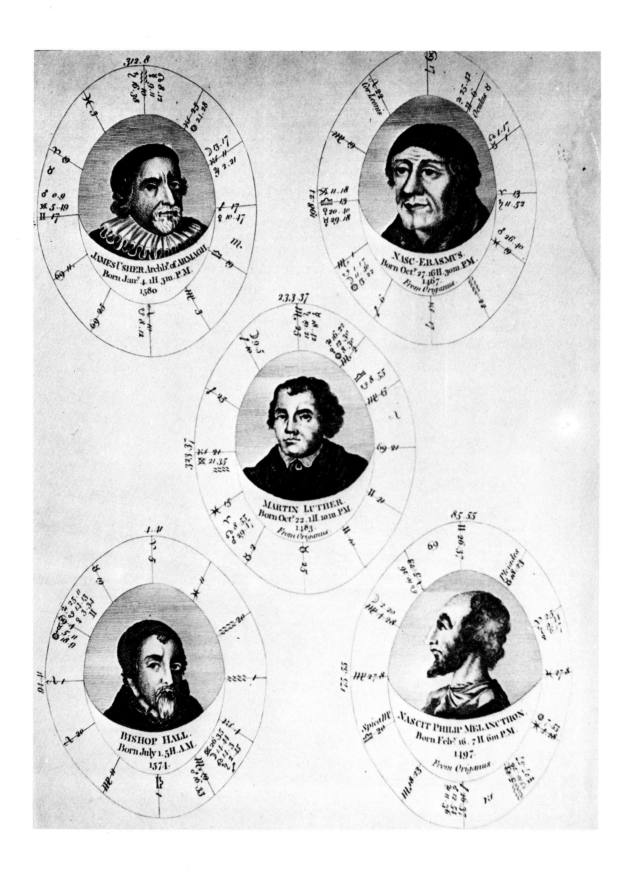

39. *Taurus in the fixed stars. (From Bevis).*

40. *Taurus weighed down by inertia, surrounded by symbols of material wealth.*

41. *Venus in her chariot. Cupid is here more as a symbol of an amorous nature, than of love. The birds drawing the chariot might well be nightingales (see page 40).*

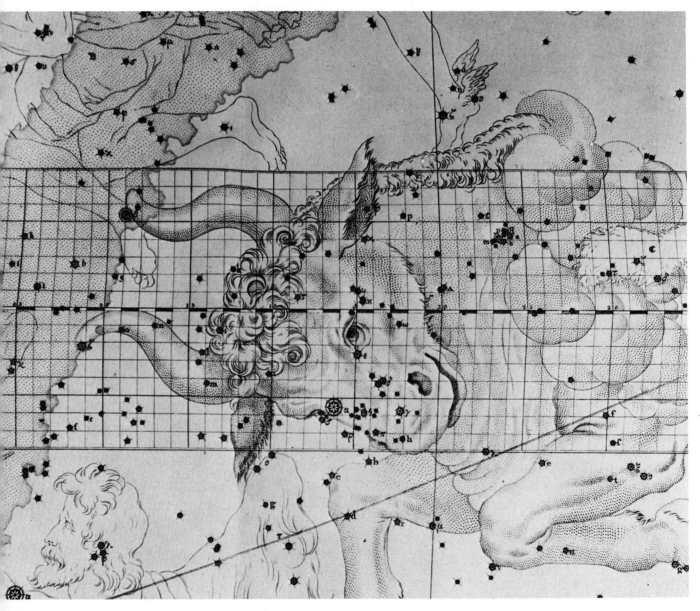

TAURUS

If this sign ascends at birth, or is posited in the sun or moon's place, it usually renders a person with a broad brow, thick lips, dark curling hair, of qualities somewhat brutal and unfeeling; melancholy, and slow to anger; but, when once enraged, violent and furious, and difficult to be appeased. (1579:*1*)

Here we see how the pugnacity of Taurus is often emphasised in astrological descriptions, perhaps in order to link the type with the traditional bull. We note that the Taurean has a violent streak, much as the bull may demonstrate himself to have, when he is baited, or when his pastures are encroached upon. 'Taurus the Bull' comes to mind so easily that we rarely ask if it is really fair to equate the Taurean with a bull. The type is slow in his movements, deliberate, and may indeed become violent when enraged, but he has many qualities which do not remind us of a bull – as for example a love of clowning, and a sense of humour. Indeed, few of the traditional descriptions of the type would appear to draw a picture of the bull, either in terms of psychology or in terms of appearance:

40

An upright, tall, straight Body either in Man or Woman, the complexion Sanguine, not clear, but obscure and dark, long Arms, but many times the Hands and Feet short and very fleshy: a dark Hair, almost black; a strong, active Body, a good piercing hazle Eye, and wanton, and of perfect sight, of excellent understanding, and judicious in worldly affairs. (1647:*2*)

This is no picture of a bull, though it must be admitted that the 'wanton' eye, so neatly tucked away in this nutshell description, does in fact

42. *Horoscope of the astrologer William Lilly who had Sun, Mercury and Venus in Taurus.*

43. *The Bull as an emblem of Taurus. This is from one of Lilly's books on predictions: it is likely that the Bull is intended to stand for Ireland.*

44. *The native of Taurus is supposed to look like a bull though many Taureans are extremely beautiful.*

hint at the connection with the bull in a certain sexual connotation. How come, we might well ask ourselves, that the reliable, solid, materialistic figure of Taurus, the most practical and down to earth of all the zodical types, should figure as 'wanton'? Let us examine a reliable modern description of our type, in which all the strength of Taurus is admirably revealed:

The chief characteristic of the highly developed Taurean is his stability of character and of purpose. He is the steadfast mind, unshaken in adversity, and his the power of quiet persistence in the face of difficulties. He has found his true position with regard to the Universe, and that position is the centre. Identified with the Self of all selves, one with the very heart of things, he refuses to be hustled or hurried or frightened or pushed into any false position, either mental or physical; and generally excels in work requiring a sense of true proportion and a just appreciation of relative values. He thoroughly understands the importance of system, method and order, enjoys routine and regularity, and often shows constructive ability, especially in matters concerning the foundations and beginnings of enterprise. He works best when spurred by necessity or inspired by the love of others, and especially by love of his wife and family, and in hard circumstances his patience and perseverance are marvellous. He generally has a horror of debt, and shows much care and prudence in the administration of affairs, succeeding particularly well in businesses such as banking, life assurance and trust work of all kinds. The office of acting as mainstay or prop in material ways is peculiarly congenial to the type, and it consequently provides many ideal trustees and guardians – people who will make large sacrifices of time and energy, rather than fail those who have confided in them. The widow and the fatherless find in them towers of strength, and the commercial integrity which qualifies them for such posts also fits them for many kinds of public office. People of this type suit subordinate positions, junior partnerships, and so forth, preferring to have boundaries and limits set them by someone in supreme authority, for obedience comes easy to them

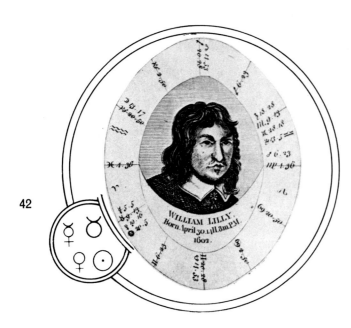

42

43

44

38

45. The female Taurean in all her sensuous beauty, alongside the more primitive Taurean male. (From Varley).

46. Venus by Giorgione (Dresden). Taurus inherits from Venus a love for the sensuous, as well as an urge to take things easy.

47. Another Taurean beauty. (From Varley).

45

47

46

when they have once given in their allegiance or accepted an office... (1911:*3*)

This pillar of society, the salt of the commercial earth, shows no sign of the 'wanton' eye. Yet if we pursue this matter a little further, we shall find that it helps towards a deeper understanding of the sign. If he is anything, the Taurean is possessive; he clings to that which is material, and he values the world in material terms. On this level he is indeed the bull, guarding that which is his own, be it his pathetic strip of field, or his vast acres, his single cow or his herd. He is possessive, certainly, but even in his possessiveness he is gentle, 'of excellent understanding, and judicious in worldly affairs'. This gentleness, which is his proper nature when he is not baited, springs from Venus, for it is this planet, the goddess of love, the patroness of the arts, which rules our Taurus, and Venus is both gentle and soft. Now, yoke together in an impossible union the stolid masculine materiality of the bull and the gentle feminine harmony of Venus, and you have the Taurean. This impossible union is both hard and soft, hard because of the bull, and soft because of the goddess:

Venus is a feminine planet...author of mirth and conviviality alluring to procreation and to the propogation of the species. When she ascends at a nativity, she gives a handsome, well-formed but not tall, stature; complexion fair and lovely, bright sparkling eyes of a dark hazle or black, the face round, regular, smooth, and engaging; the hair light brown, hazle or chestnut, shining and plentiful; the body regular and well-proportioned; and of a neat, smart, and airy, disposition, generally with dimples in the cheeks or chin, and often in both; the eye wandering, and naturally amorous; in motion light and nimble; in voice, soft, easy, sweet, and agreeable, inclined to amorous conversation, and early engagements in love. (1795:*4*)

And so this is why the Taurean bull is so often 'light and nimble' when one would expect him to be heavy and clumsy, and this is why our sign so often produces such beautiful people. The gentleness of Venus, and her beauty, linked with the strength of the bull – who could

wish for anything more?

Again, we must not forget that Venus is the patron of the arts, for this accounts for the fact that the energy of the bull is frequently harnessed to the spirit of Venus, and the Taurean is creative. The Taurean delights in the arts, especially in music and painting, and he delights to be in his own home, among his own children, even if he does tend to regard them as possessions. Beyond this, however, he likes to be left alone in his field, lording it over his own, not caring over much for other people. It is hard to disturb him from this placid or creative circle, because he is quite convinced that he is right in what he is doing: 'Who knows, or thinks he knows, the most?' asks one nineteenth-century astrological riddle – and the answer could only be 'Oh, Taurus!' Indeed, some sixteen centuries earlier, Ptolemy had words to say about this aspect of the Taurean nature, about what the astrologers call his 'fixity':

Fixed signs make men just, void of flattery, constant, firm, prudent, patient, laborious, rigid, continent, mindful of injuries, followers of what they begin, contentious, ambitious, seditious, covetous, obstinate.

(c.2nd Century A.D.:*5*)

So our more gentle picture of Taurus is changing a little – Taurus is headstrong, opinionated, and obstinate. But perhaps this is all for the good when you really do know what you are about, when you stand at the hub of the universe, when you are creative, and when you want to get on with something. It is best to be right, when you have something you want to do. Ditherers, and those who do not know, rarely *produce* anything – and Taureans always produce something. He is productive and possessive, of people as well as of ideas, but his general fixity is relieved by a strong power of joking. This joking, and love of clowning, comes from Venus, for it is Venus who rules all that is convivial and gentle, all that is beautiful, and once more the unlikely union produces a strange image – that of a laughing bull. Yet the conviviality, which shows itself in the humour and in love of good things, is bound to be present in one ruled by Venus, the goddess who

48

49

'denotes gentle showers in winter, and temperate heat in summer', a goddess for whom even the trees are gentle: the sweet apple, for example, the white rose, the white sycamore and the "wilde Ashe" – this perhaps because traditionally it was with ashwood that the fire was made to warm the infant Jesus. Yet among the animals associated with Venus, we find more hints of that wanton streak, of that which 'incites to wantonnesse':

Animals under Venus. All such as are of a hot and amorous nature, as the dog, coney, bull, sheep, goat, calf, panther, and hart. Among fishes, the pilchard, gilthead, whiting, crab, dolphin and tithymallus. And among birds, the swan, water-wagtail, swallow, pelican, nightingale, pigeon, sparrow, turtledove, stock-dove, crow, eagle, burgander, partridge, thrush, blackbird, pye, wren... (1795:*6*)

Forgiving the presence of the herb 'tithymallus' among the fishes – a herb, in fact, which one authority tells us will 'purge furiously' – and incidentally wondering how the pilchard happens to be of a 'hot and amorous' nature, we do see in these associations a tendency of Venus to run wild. Here then is the clue to the 'wanton' eye of our bull!

Venus did indeed have a bad reputation in the early almanacs, particularly when she became too much involved with the needs of the body, and most early woodcuts show Venus naked, sometimes admiring herself in a mirror, sometimes besporting herself naked in a bath with a young man, and in this aspect she was the patroness of whoring. It is not surprising that Venus in excess will disturb the placid nature of the Taurean, throw the bull half off balance, so to speak. The balance between the two who comprise this unlikely union is a perilous one at the best of times: there is the creative spirit of Venus immured in the inertia of a heavy body – by all rulerships the Taurean is a nightingale who wants to be free, but which finds itself caged in a body much like that of a bull. When the nightingale struggles for freedom the delicate balance may be disturbed, or the nightingale may rage in impotent despair and lose his sweetness. We all know these despairing Taureans, and indeed a Taurean in this state of being is a frightening spectacle, usually described by astrologers as the 'primitive type', by which they mean a Taurean lacking the sweetness of gentle Venus:

The primitive specimen naturally prefers to keep his good things to himself and often by seeking to save his life loses it; for excess of vitality stored up, instead of flowing for the benefit of others, is a danger, and not an advantage to the owner. At the early stages our Taurean, instead of finding his own centre in the Divine Centre of the Universe, is self-centred in the ordinary sense of the word, and quite incapable of seeing anyone's point of view but his own. His steadfast nature and splendid persistence only show as a mulish obstinacy and a pigheaded determination to hold his own. Tranquility and restfulness are represented by laziness and sloth, and the inherent loyalty characteristic of the developed type as well as its strength and solidity of character, are only recognisable in an ignorant and foolish dislike of change, and a dogged disinclination to strenuous exertion of any kind. The primitive Taurean is absurdly overcautious and exasperatingly deliberate; and his filial devotion to his Mother Earth and gratitude for her gifts are often perverted to a gross materialism accompanied by much self-indulgence, which saps the energy and leads to mental stagnation. He is never aggressive in battle, and avoids it if possible, but when pushed to the wall, or persistently goaded, will sometimes astonish his opponent by an outburst of fury dangerous while it lasts, but quickly succeeded by resumption of stolidity. Even at this early stage, the sense of humour is conspicuous, and although his little joke may take some time in the making, it is usually a genuine achievement of its kind, even if it hardly rises above the level of the grotesque and is distinguished rather for its breadth than for its depth. (1911:7)

Fortunately, the primitive side of Taurus is applicable to few, for generally the type is of 'excellent understanding', and on the side of the Venusian angels. The emphasis of interpretation put upon the ruling planet Venus has changed considerably since she was the 'ruler

48. *The primitive Taurean, who loves the earth, and constructive work.*
49. *Venus, the ruler over music, food and the lascivious life.*
50. *A horoscope of the Taurean author Balzac.*
51. *Portrait of Balzac. Taurus often inclines to be corpulent, particularly around the neck.*

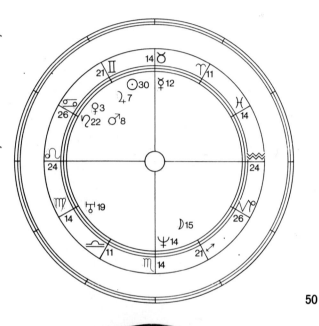

50

51

of whores', one who would 'desire oft to commune of lust and love, and covet oft sweetmeats and drinks as wine and be oft drunken, and oft desire lechery and the beholding of fair women, and the women of men in likewise, and use fleshly lust oftentimes'. The emphasis has changed, and Venus is nowadays seen in terms of what the nineteenth-century astrologers called 'esoteric astrology'. Here one of them speaks of this deeper Venus:

In trying to define the inner nature of any planet, we are really endeavouring to grasp the fundamental principles underlying the whole universe. The mind can only understand so much of external objects as it finds reflected within itself; and anything not so reflected, or only half reflected, will be either wholly or partially misunderstood. The humanity of today is imperfect; its evolution is not finished; and therefore the cosmic principles, reflected in an imperfect mirror, appear distorted and only half-intelligible. The planet Venus, in particular, has suffered from this imperfect comprehension; and its lowest reference to sex in the physical body, and that as lust rather than as love, has often been mistaken for its fullest and most radical signification. At its best, the planet is as high above this as the heavens are above the earth; and it is scarcely going too far to say that the man of to-day does not and cannot understand it... (1904:8)

Here, then, we touch upon the conditions which raise the heavy earth of bull Taurus, the salt of humanity, to a level where he may be creative. Seen in the light of 'esoteric astrology' the problem as to how something so weighty, so involved with inertia, may also be an advanced spirit, ceases to have much relevance. The purpose of the Taurean life is to reach the higher vibration of the Venusian nature within the being: the lower nature, the involvement with sex, the identification with the body, is only too clearly evident. What is not so evident, but what is clearly *felt* in all Taurean lives, is the need to remove to a higher level of vibration where these splendid energies, normally dedicated to the life of the body, may be utilized in the services of the spirit.

52. The Bull. (From Bewick). The slow heavy nature is hard to associate with the rhythm-loving Taurean.

53. 'Peasants dancing' by Breugel (Vienna). Taureans love music and dancing, and the sign rules over peasants. They are fond of clowning, and earthy, bawdy humour.

In certain respects, therefore, the tradition attached to Taurus is a little unfair. A modern astrologer concedes that there is an 'apparent anomaly' in Taurus; from the point of view of morality one must admit that it stands rather low, and even manifests more than average criminal tendencies, yet at the same time it is capable of high development.* He explains this anomaly in terms of our studying the principle of Taurus from below, in its material condition:

Life, as it were, is kindled in Aries, accumulates power in Taurus, and then flows freely into the common sign Gemini, where we may suggest that the Divine Ideas take distinctive shape and become the differentiated intellectual Archetypes of all that comes into existence in the objective worlds. (1928:9)

Taurus is therefore the reservoir of power, and the Taurean is one who is quite clearly faced with a *material* condition weighing down the spirit, which makes the young spirit wish to cling to the illusions presented by the material world. A spirit who can see the degree of this illusion, 'the puppet show' as the Tibetans call it, is already in a state where he may leave it behind, and go on to higher things. This is why the Taurean existence may be described as a fight with inertia, for the whole of the material world is one which gives rise to inertia: the full weight of the material world may be felt only by a Taurean who struggles with his inner nature, which by a strange paradox is also the outer world! The life of the Taurean has a Promethian quality about it, for it is based on the age-old epic of the struggles of a nightingale to free itself from a cage!

* *The Zodiac and the Soul. f. 17 ff. C. E. O. Carter.*

52

54. *Gemini in the fixed stars.* (From Bevis).
55. *Gemini the twins. Geminians are fond of gesticulating with the hands.*
56. *The dual Geminian, with his tendency to do so many things at the same time. Gemini rules rapid communications.*
57. *Mercury and its rulership over the arts – painting, sculpture and astronomy. Many Geminians are creative.*

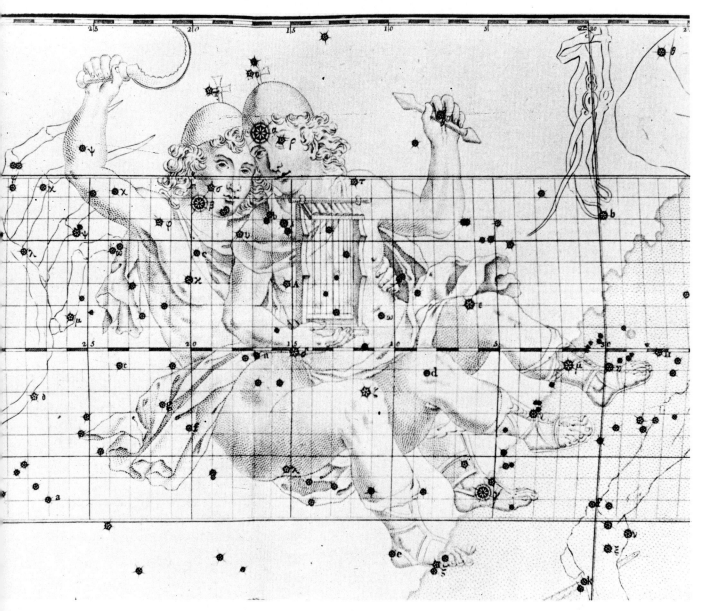

GEMINI

55

Sun in Gemini confers a well-proportioned body; complexion sanguine; hair brown; of a good, affable, and kind disposition, rather deficient in firmness and resolution; and not particularly fortunate. (1879:*1*)

Sad that one of so kind a disposition, and one who is generally happy, should be 'not particularly fortunate', but this is so. At the same time we find that in certain fields – in literature, in acting, in public relations and so on – the Geminian excels and is held by many to be very fortunate indeed. It is possible to think of the Geminian as being unfortunate for two reasons: first because he is so restless, born under a wandering star; and secondly because he secretly considers himself to be meant for better things than life usually provides. He realizes more than most that life is free, and because of this he makes many demands of people and of the world at large: inevitably, of course, this leads to frustration, for few people will give freely all the time. The Geminian will therefore go around sincerely believing that he is not getting his just deserts, and considering himself unfortunate:

> The primitive Geminian will take from anyone; not merely accepting but exacting as his due, sympathy, attention, consideration, admiration, time, energy and pecuniary assistance: in fact, anything and everything that will feed his egotism or further his physical and intellectual development. (1911:*2*)

It was surely a stroke of genius by the ancient astrologers to make Gemini rule over sparrows, who are famous for their cheeky begging and genteel thieving. We must not be surprised that

56

58. *Peter Pan and Wendy. Some Geminians have a reputation for not wishing to grow up: most Geminians retain their youth well into old age.*

58

one who makes so many demands should be frequently turned away without the crumbs, and should perhaps consider himself unfortunate. And yet, whether the Geminian gets his crumbs or his whole loaf of bread, there is another reason why the Geminian may consider himself unfortunate:

A constant demand for entertainment, novelty and excitement results in a tendency to shirk uncongenial duties, and leave 'the trivial round, the common task' as much as possible to others. Routine work of any kind is particularly resented as an affliction, and until the advantage of regular and punctual attention to minor details in housekeeping, office work, etc., is intellectually understood and appreciated, the Geminian doomed to such labour feels like a bird in a cage, and expends far more energy in beating against the bars with his wings than would suffice to fulfil his obligations three times over. The root of all such unhappiness and rebellion is generally the secret conviction that he or she, however heedless and incompetent, is meant for better things, and is consequently thrown away on drudgery of any kind. (1911:*3*)

The Geminian, therefore, is not so much actually an unfortunate person; rather he more often than not *regards* himself as being unfortunate. The quickwitted Mercury is the planet which rules over our Gemini, and he also has rulership over Wednesday: we all know that Wednesday's child is traditionally 'full of woe', and we may consider that this in itself accounts for the Geminian sense of being unfortunate. But Mercury also presides over Saturday night, and in this double rulership we touch the very nature of our dual sign. There are two sides to Gemini, which is why the glyph for the sign shows two upright lines linked together – one side which is serious, perhaps even sad, and another side which is very much 'Saturday night' in its longing for enjoyment, fun and carouse:

a strong, active Body, a good piercing hazle Eye, and wanton, and of perfect sight, of excellent understanding, and judicious in worldly affairs. (1647:*4*)

So our Gemini is a little 'wanton', perhaps

addicted to making every night a Saturday night, but he is also serious at times, being possessed of a brilliant mind and a delightful facility of expression – this because he is ruled over by that live-wire Mercury:

he represents a man of subtill and politick braine, intellect, and cogitation; an excellent disputant or Logician, arguing with learning and discretion, and using much eloquence in his speech, a searcher into all kinds of Mysteries, Learning, sharpe and witty, learning almost any thing without a Teacher; ambitious of being exquisite in every Science, desirous naturally of travell and seeing foraign parts; a man of unwearied fancie, curious in the search of any occult knowledge, able by his owne *Genius* to produce wonders; given to Divination and the more secret knowledge; if he turne Merchant no man exceeds him in way of Trade or invention of new ways whereby to obtain wealth. (1647:5)

Thus we have a picture of the 'good' Geminian sufficient to satisfy the ego of any Geminian, but we must remember that Mercury may be under pressure in the horoscope; when he is good he is very, very good, but when he is bad, he is horrid – the 'author of subtilty, tricks and devices, perjury, &.'

A troublesome wit, a kinde of Herenetick* man, his tongue and Pen against every man, wholly bent to foole his estate and time in prating and trying nice conclusions to no purpose; a great lyar, boaster, pratler, busibody, false, a tale-carrier, given to wicked Arts, as Necromancy, and such like ungodly knowledges; easie of beleefe, an asse or very ideot, constant in no place or opinion, cheeting and theeving everywhere; a newesmonger, pretending all manner of knowledge, but guilty of no true or solid learning; a trifler; a meere frantick fellow; if he prove a Divine, than a meer verball fellow, frothy, of no judgement, easily perverted, constant in nothing, but idle words and bragging. (1647:6)

Hard words, but necessary to show how low our type may fall when he is not of a 'good, affable, and kind disposition'. But perhaps the professions listed by our own hard author as being suitable for Geminians reveals something

* *The meaning of this word is obscure, but somehow delightfully apt!*

59. Oliver Twist cleaning the boots of that low-quality Geminian, the Artful Dodger. When under pressure, Mercury tends to express itself through either dubious or criminal activities.

60. The detective Sherlock Holmes, whom some astrologers regard as being a perfect symbol of the highly evolved, intellectual Geminian.

59

60

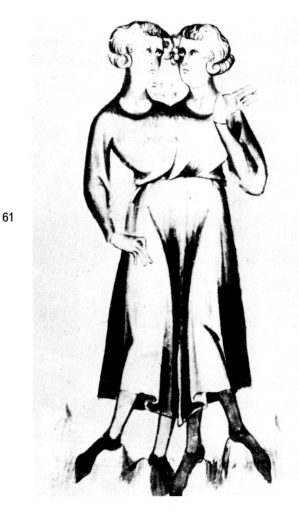

61

of a more capable nature, something of the real quality of his mind, something of that amazing versatility which has led to him being described as the zodiacal Jack of all trades, the one who may be all things to all men:

He generally signifies all literated men, Philosophers, Mathematicians, Astrologians, Merchants, Secretaries, Scriveners, Diviners, Sculptors, Poets, Orators, Advocates, Schoolmasters, Stationers, Printers, Exchangers of Money, Atturneys, Emperours, Embassadours, Commissioners, Clerks, Artificers, generally Accomptants, Solicitors, sometimes Theeves, pratling muddy Ministers, busie Sectaries, and they unlearned; Grammarians, Taylors, Carriers, Messengers, Foot-men, Userers. (1647:7)

One gets the impression that this seventeenth-century astrologer did not much like men of the cloth, but his list runs fairly true even to this day, for Mercury produces the clever intellectual, and Gemini does rule over literary men, men of great intellect, as well as 'all cunning creatures'. An example from a more recent pen backs this up for we find that the intellect of the type is emphasised:

Flexible, irritable, worrying, self contained, nervous, vacillating, see both sides to every question, versatile, changeable, clever, inventive, original, fond of knowledge for its own sake, always want to know why, subtle, brilliant wit, fond of puns, puzzles, and conjuring tricks, sceptical schemers, capable of pure abstract thought, mathematical, coldly scientific and dispassionate, may be dishonest. (1922:8)

It has taken a couple of centuries of Geminian influences, in the *persona* of the U.S.A. and London (both under Gemini), plus the general conning and superficiality to which our civilization tends, for astrologers to recognize and appreciate fully the characteristics of Gemini. Mere intellect, restlessness, hustle and bustle, all beloved by Geminians, are nowadays somehow regarded as virtues of a kind, and we find in modern books an enthusiasm for the Geminian type, which is quite lacking in earlier astrological writings:

It is pre-eminently the Sign connected

Taglia Cantoni. Fracasso.

62

with the concrete mind, or that part of the mind which deals with facts and figures rather than with ideals and experiments. It is the Sign of reason and logic, and Geminians excel all others in their ability to grasp conceptions clearly and logically. Hazy or sentimental thinking, leading to loose or inaccurate conclusions, are particularly distasteful to them, and, while able to deal with abstractions, and usually very interested in literature and art, they are always capable of examining things from the rational standpoint without any emotional bias. They are more matter-of-fact than sentimental, and admire and like brain and cleverness. They are nearly always mentally active themselves and are quick at repartee, being bright and energetic conversationalists, good debaters, and keen at argument. There is much mental vivacity and agility... The faults of the Sign are lack of concentration and the tendency to take on too many projects and enterprises, so that they have 'too many irons in the fire', and leave things unfinished. Only when this diffusive tendency is overcome can the Sign get the most from its fine intellectual powers. There is lack of decision and a good deal of wavering and difficulty in making up the mind. The Geminian often excels in detail, and may lose himself in it, failing to 'see the wood on account of the trees.' Emotionally there is a distinct tendency to egoism, hardness, and selfishness, Gemini people being too mental to develop warmth of heart. Even when the rest of the nativity shows generosity of feeling, it cannot manifest freely and easily through Gemini. There is often too great a liking for introspection, with resultant self-centredness and discontent. There is sometimes flippancy and irreverence. (1925:9) So we know that the Geminian is intellectually agile, mentally orientated, and perhaps rather cold in matters of the heart, but we have not yet noted what the Geminian looks like. In the astrological tradition the native tends to look a little like the animal associated with the sign, and because of this we find that Geminians are often rather striking, for Gemini rules over many strange creatures. The sign rules over

61. *The dual Geminian from a fifteenth century manuscript. (British Museum).*

62. *Two men in masks fencing, by Callot. Gemini rules fencing, both the sport and the verbal equivalent: Geminians are fond of playing a part and are usually expert at 'wearing masks of their own making'.*

63. *The theatre at Versailles. Gemini rules the theatre, as well as Versailles.*

64

65

sparrows, as we have noted, and over the monkey, as well as the flea, so one would expect the Geminian type to have some resemblance to a monkey or a flea. The artist John Varley, who also wrote on astrology, had no difficulty in deciding that the portrait of the 'ghost of a flea' which his friend the visionary William Blake drew from life, looked like a Geminian (figure 66), for indeed he published this portrait in a later book as a fair image of the Geminian. On the appearance of Gemini, Varley had a few well-chosen words:

> Gemini, though a beautiful and human sign yet occasionally gives to persons born when it is rising a strong resemblance in the head and neck to the characteristic forms of goats, kids and deer; and therefore, being bicorporal sign, or one of plurality, in very ancient times it was represented by two kids; but subsequently, the human character of the sign has been recognised by the introduction of the *Twins*, representing the two stars Castor and Pollux. (1828:*10*)

Perhaps to liken the appearance of the Geminian to that of a goat may seem a little unfair, but there *is* often such a relation, even though the Geminian is usually attractive, and even though they retain their beauty and youthful appearance throughout life. What faults they have appear to be emotional or spiritual ones:

> *Gemini* gives a delicate, strait, well-composed, and well-made Body, bright clear eyes, good sight, and piercing, long arms, long hands and feet, large breast, brown hair, good wit, fluent tongue, and apt to discourse; yet a man of no great fidelity. (1679:*11*)

And so here we touch upon the root of the spiritual weakness: 'a man of no great fidelity' – and this alone accounts for why so many Geminians consider themselves unfortunate. The Geminian will be unfaithful to his loved one because he rarely loves deeply, and always has his goat-like eyes on other pastures green. He desires variety and duality, and loves the excitement of intrigue. For similar reasons he will be 'unfaithful' to himself and to projects he begins, finding it difficult to bring them to completion and being too anxious to get on with the next thing. Because of this lack of

64. *Gemini rules London. With this figure (published in 1651) the astrologer Lilly predicted the Great Fire of London some years before it occurred.*
65. *Sarah Bernhardt, a typical Geminian actress.*

66. *The Ghost of a flea, drawn by William Blake for the astrologer Varley. Varley decided that the flea looked like a Geminian. (From* Varley).
67. *A kinder version of the Geminian. (From* Varley).

'great fidelity' the Geminian constantly invites trouble on to his own head, One should never ask a Geminian to undertake a long-term project, and while he may be held a good friend, a charming and delightful companion, one should rarely trust him with a valuable thing, such as a heart.

Yet it is still possible that we have not been quite fair to the Geminian: we have likened him first to a sparrow, then to a goat; we have termed him unfortunate, and now we say that he is not to be trusted. Yet his keynote in the cosmic scale is that of *Joy*, and he has a delightful nature: how otherwise could one be proud to be born under Gemini? The astrologer Alan Leo, kind to most of the signs, is particularly kind to Gemini – presumably because Fire types get on well with Air types. He addresses himself to the Geminian in the personal button-holing style of the Leo:

You have good mental abilities and an active and flexible mind. This is one of the intellectual signs, and those who are born under it usually have abilities for writing, studying, speaking or thinking. You are fond of books and reading, you can learn easily from books or lectures, you can apply your mind to a variety of subjects and are ingenious and inventive. You are suitable for receiving a good education and are adapted for almost any literary pursuit or clerical work. You have good reasoning powers, a thoughtful mind, and are fluent either of speech or pen. You have ability for languages and science and are also fond of travel. You have comprehensiveness of mind and a quick adaptability to various pursuits and studies, but you are

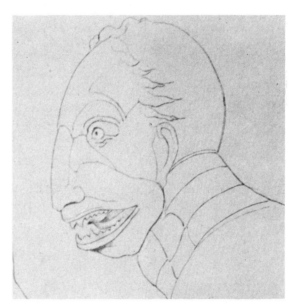

66

67

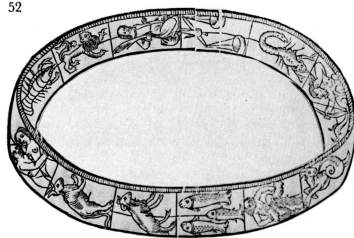

68. *"Posters at Trouville" by Dufy, a Geminian artist. Gemini rules advertising. (Musee National d'Art Moderne, Paris).*
69. *Zodiacal man, from a fifteenth century manuscript on astrology. (British Museum).*

68

somewhat lacking in concentration and perseverance. You are rather irresolute, uncertain, and changeable at times, do not feel sure of yourself and may even hold or express contradictory opinions. You are liable to worry and irritation, and are easily upset by little annoyances. You are kind, humane and sympathetic, but you know what it is to have fits of shyness, nervousness, and reserve, when you withdraw into yourself. Reason and understanding are your strong faculties, but you are liable to lack continuity and strength of will. (1910:*12*)

On a different plane, but no less relevant, another modern astrologer explains some of the faults of the Geminian in terms of the basic egoism which underlies almost all Geminian behaviour. Of course, we are all egoists, but there is a coldness about the Geminian, removed in his mental tower, which makes his egoism more deeply felt and more evident, though we must admit that the explanation of Geminian selfhood applies to us all:

Deity manifesting on the physical plane must express the Self in terms of that plane, limited and bounded by physical conditions; must build up a personality – an efficient body – by means of which expression is possible. The building of such a personality is, in its essence, egoism; *i.e.*, the separating of a part of the greater self, the process of allowing it to become an 'own self' something different from all other selves; a process which, like many other forms of birth or of growth, involves pain, and in a certain limited sense, loss to the parent self. (1911:13)

And thus the human condition is explained –

we are caught in an aspect of time, and the
self is an illusion which fetters us. In this
explanation of Geminian selfhood we find also
an explanation of the cosmic illusion, the reason
for this joy and sorrow during a ridiculously
short period of seventy-five years or so. The
duality underlying the Geminian is emphasised
in all accounts of the type:

Many Gemini persons may be said to be
double. One trait of character seems to
contradict another trait – in other words, they
have a dual nature in active operation. They
want to travel, and they want to stay at home.
They wish to study, and they wish to play.
They are happy and unhappy, satisfied and
dissatisfied at the same time. They are in love
and not in love; warm and cold in one breath.
The Gemini people do not fly quite so high as
the other denizens of the Air Triplicity,
because the twins are not always agreed upon
the destination. This contradiction causes a
state of nervousness which is very hard to
overcome. Gemini people are extremely
affectionate and generous, very courteous and
kind to all. They are proud of birth, and have
a great deal of family pride. They are not a
selfish or penurious people. They are thoughtful of the poor, and very sympathetic with the
suffering. They are fond of the arts and
sciences, are great readers and good talkers,
and very quick to see the point of a story or
joke. These people are not usually successful
wage-earners, and frequently give away as
fast as they can earn...

Gemini people should learn to keep their feet
and hands still. The restlessness of these
members is a true sympton of the restlessness
of the spirit, and the determination to conquer
a physical expression very quickly has its
influence upon the subjective mind. (1894:*14*)

This is perhaps a fine sentiment upon which to
round off our survey of this restless type the
Geminian. The moralizing may well be out of
place, however, for if he heeds anything at all
it can only be expressed in terms of a contradiction: basically, the type needs an audience
and yet at the same time he needs to be left
alone to pursue his own interest. Happy is he
who can resolve this paradox in himself!

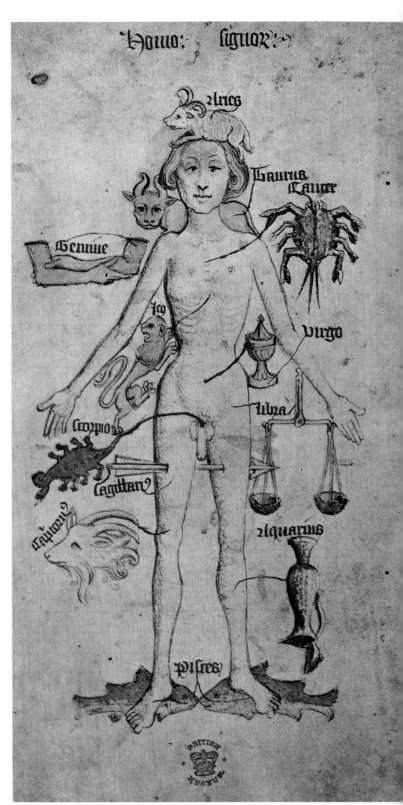

69

70. *Cancer the Crab, in the fixed stars.
(From Bevis).*
71. *Cancer the Crab, looking more like a
crayfish, as it tended to do in early
astrological books.*
72. *The imaginative Cancer, lost in
watery dreams.*
73. *Moon, the ruler over fishermen, and
women, and all sublunary change. In
modern astrology she rules the
subconscious.*

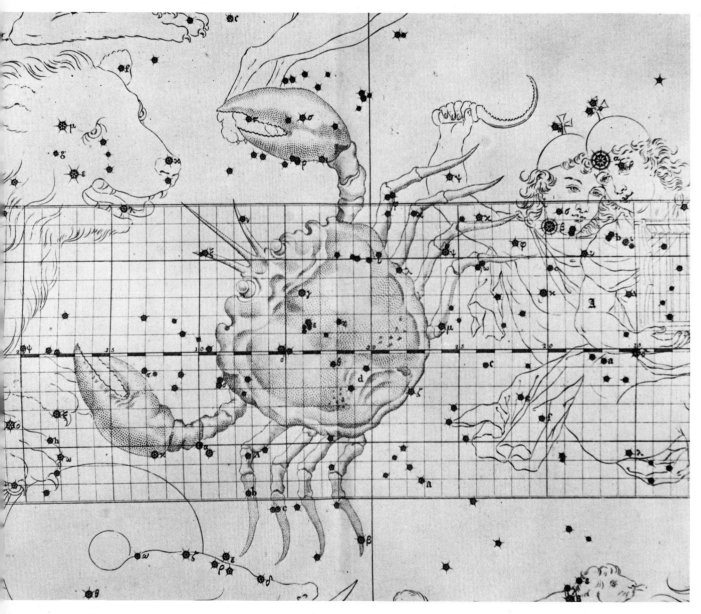

CANCER

Cancer gives moderate stature, generally larger from the middle upward than below: face full and round with a white or pale and delicate complexion, nose short and rounded, hair light brown, and small greyish or bluish eyes: rather effeminate and seldom of strong constitution: females prolific, timid, and dull. (1905:1)

Those last three words, damning as they are, sum up the traditional image of Cancer only too well. Fortunately for the Cancerian, the traditional image is not based on truth: some Cancerians may well be timid and dull, but most of them are not, and in order to understand our sign aright we must find out why the traditional image is wrong, and then see what Cancerians are *really* like.

Unwittingly, perhaps, a seventeenth-century description of the places which fall under the rulership of Cancer points to the centre of our problem:

Places. The Sea, great Rivers, Navigable Waters; but in the Inland Countries it notes places neer Rivers, Brooks, Springs, Wels, Sellars, in Houses Wash-houses, Marsh grounds, Ditches with Rushes, Sedges, Sea banks, Trenches, Cisternes. (1647:2)

All of which leaves us in no doubt that Cancer is of a watery nature, 'Watry, Cold, Moyst', as the same authority insists. Cancer is indeed a water sign, and what is more she falls under the rule of the watery Moon, who traditionally has influence over all connexions with the sea and with water:

Sailors, Fishermen, Fish-mongers, Brewers, Tapsters, Vintners... Ale-wives, Malsters, Drunkards, Oister-wives, Fisher-women...

72

73

74. *A colour print entitled 'Mildew blasting Ears of Corn', by the Cancerian mystic, painter and poet William Blake. For all its reputation as an 'ordinary sign', Cancer produces remarkable genius. Blake has his Moon in Cancer on the fixed star Sirius, as well as a Cancerian Ascendant. The insistent rhythm of the print is typical of Cancerian art, as are the colours. (British Museum).*

74

Midwives, Nurses, &. Hackney-men, Water-men, Water-bearers. (1647:*3*)

And so this watery Moon pours its energy into the watery Cancer, and the result is virtually pure water. Now the thing about water is that it is colourless in itself, and therefore takes its identity from the things around it – water will reflect on the surface, will transmit from the bottom, and its powers of reflection are affected only if the surface of the water is disturbed. The thing about the Moon is that it takes its identity from the Sun: the waxing and the waning of the Moon which has been taken for so long as a symbol of mutability, of inconstancy, is on a fairly prosaic level merely a record of its changing relationship to the Sun. This is why the Moon has become in astrological doctrine the symbol of receptivity in human beings: she in herself represents the subconscious, and is dangerously near having no 'fortune' of her own:

Her influence, in itself, is neither fortunate nor unfortunate, but as she happens to fall in with the configurations of the other planets, and is then either malevolent or otherwise as those aspects happen to be... If she be well dignified at the nativity, the native will be of soft engaging manners and disposition, a lover of the polite arts, and of an ingenious imagination... If the Moon be ill dignified at the birth, the native will then be slothful, indolent, and of no forecast; given up to a drunken, disorderly, beggarly, life, hating labour, or any kind of business or employment. (1795:*4*)

Thus water reflects, and the Moon 'reflects', and so it is not unlikely that watery Cancer, under the rays of the Moon, will also reflect. The fact that Cancer is a kind of colourless reservoir (and significantly, a symbol of what we now call the subconscious) proves our point, and also explains the general inability of the textbook descriptions of Cancer to pinpoint the truth, to dismiss those born under Cancer as 'timid and dull', when in fact they are not timid, and are not dull in the least, any more than they resemble crabs!

If we may take it that the thirty degrees of Cancer represent an incredibly sensitive stretch of the zodiac which is seeking to reflect some force or other in order to take on an identity of its own, then we will see that anything in that part of the zodiac, from a fly to a planet, will be magnified, transmitted and reflected in a most powerful manner. Almost any student of astrology will agree with this: Cancer is sensitive, and Cancer will reflect! What is so frequently overlooked by astrologers is the simple fact that in these thirty sensitive degrees there are always particularly strong forces at work. If the Sun is in the sign, then always the conscious mind of the personality is sensitive; if the Moon, then always the subconscious mind of the personality is sensitive. If the Ascendant is in Cancer, then the whole vibration of the person is highly sensitive on every level, and in a variable manner. Even the degrees, when grouped in fives, show sensitivity and a wide variety of expression:

Asc. From 1 to 5 degrees, shows a wise wary person, a good orator, deceitful, jealous of everybody, fearful, and always mistrusting the worst things.

Asc. From 5 to 10 degrees, shews one of a good tongue, bold adventurous nature, yet doing all things with advice and consideration; subject to affront everybody, but unwilling to receive any, a man conceited of his own wisdom and abilities, and to undervalue all others.

Asc. From 10 to 15 degrees, signify a good orator, one sober, serious, and of a melancholy disposition, crafty, subtil, and deceitful; if Saturn is here, his craft is beyond measure; if Mars, he is impudent in mischief; if Sun, he accounts it his glory, yet Sun much meliorates the manners of the native, and makes him ambitious of doing worthy acts, not so much for the love as for the honor of them; if Moon be here, the man is more worthy, but very mutable in his resolves; if Jupiter the man is honestly religious, and sober.

Asc. From 15 to 20 degrees, it shews a melancholy person, envious, proud, stubborn, self-willed, not delightful to hear reason, but only what feeds and nourishes ill humours; of a sad and timorous disposition, yet outbraving the whole world.

Asc. From 20 to 25 degrees, gives the native

75. Durer 'Adoration of the Magi' (Uffizi). Cancer rules the maternal instinct, as well as the early part of childhood, when the human is most impressionable. The Magi, drawn to the Christ by a star, were astrologers.

76

77

boldness, impudence, a voluble tongue, proud, saucy, and malapert, thinking always too highly of himself, and meanly of others, aiming at great things, but falling short of them through his own rashness; great self-esteem.

Asc. From 25 to 30 degrees, signifies an active turbulent spirited person, aiming at great things, through his own prudence, joined with an industrious and unwearied spirit, commonly attaining them, shews one serious but bold; melancholy, yet undaunted, weighing matters, incredulous, believing nothing but what he knows, nor trusting farther than he tries.

And so we range through many estates, from hangman to great men, from the fearful to the ones of great self-esteem, and we scarcely find trace of the 'timid, and dull' here. Thus the sensitive nature can reflect a myriad natures into the sublunary world, and thus astrologers are hard put to give a nutshell description of the type, for the type in itself scarcely exists. Listen to one astrologer:

CANCER was rising at your birth; a sign belonging to the element water and to the cardinal or movable quality. This gives you much sensitiveness and receptivity, active feelings and emotions, and love of sensation and novelty. You have a strong domestic and social nature, warm affections, and are fond of home life. You are easily influenced by those whom you love or admire, but are apt to be cold, reserved, and distrustful to those you do not know well or whom you dislike. You have an active imagination and fancy, and often live the past over again in your mind and anticipate the future. You have much prudence and forethought, are careful and cautious, and have a good deal of tenacity and firmness. You have some natural ability for trade and business management and might gain success in this direction, as you have a sense of value and economy. You have a practical mind and put everything ultimately to the test of practical use, and with care you may make a reputation as a useful and practical person in your own line of life. You live a good deal in the senses, and at times are changeful and capricious, but you also have

78

76. *Rembrandt, who had Sun and Mercury in Cancer. Many Cancerians have proved remarkable geniuses in a wide variety of fields.*
77. *The eccentric genius Dali, whose Ascendant was on the fixed star Propus which gives eminence.*
78. *The Italian painter Modigliani had the Sun, Mercury and Venus in Cancer, two of them involved with powerful fixed stars.*

79. *Madame Blavatsky. The Ascendant is 19 degrees Cancer, exactly on the fixed star Castor.*
80. *Einstein, who has 12 degrees Cancer ascending exactly on Sirius.*
81. *Proust, the French novelist, who had Sun on the fixed star Propus.*
82. *Sigmund Freud, psychologist, who had his Ascendant in Cancer in the degree next to the fixed star Pollux.*

79

80

81

82

83

84

85

patience and perseverance... (1910:6)

Not calculated exactly to make one wish to be Cancerian, or to make a Cancerian pleased with himself, and although it is pretty fair, as astrological descriptions of the type go, it does not succeed in catching the spark which is behind much of Cancer. Actually, the word *spark* is very appropriate, as the cause of Cancerian genius gives the appearance of a group of sparks in the heavens, for these are the fixed stars gathered around the ecliptic band in that part of the zodiac which astrologers call Cancer. If the watery Cancer transmits the influences it receives with such sensitivity, then surely it will transmit the powerful forces of the fixed stars which lie inside the thirty degrees of its extent? All the other eleven signs of the zodiac hold their quota of fixed stars, but they have an identity of their own — they are not like timid Cancer, seeking for an identity, seeking to be contained, to be propped up, to be enlivened. And there is no doubt that the fixed stars liven up Cancerians, for while we find that the sign Cancer results in people of widely different temperaments, some powerful, some weak, it also results in that curious manifestation, *genius*.

From 'timid, and dull' we have talked our way finally around to genius, and we are beginning to understand just why it is possible that a sign which has a reputation for producing uninteresting people will also produce the most fascinating manifestations of human kind. This is not the place to look into the fixed star tradition,* but we may note how the meek and mild Cancerian may expand, and become the master of his many moods, when operating under the strength of a powerful force for good:

The highly evolved Cancerian is the master of many moods, both in himself and in others; for when he has fully developed the faculty of expression he is the musician to whose piping all the world must dance. His true function is to vitalise and inspire the men and women of his own generation and especially the youth of his native land, by raising their ideals; and when he takes up the harp of life he smites 'on all the chords with might', making each in turn vibrate and quiver to its fullest extent.

* *The best easily-available book to consult is Vivian Robson's Fixed Stars and Constellations.*

This type is very romantic and imaginative where the affections are concerned, though often too shy or proud to betray the fact; for ridicule is torture to the Cancerian. In consequence, the story of his love-affairs is frequently a tragic sequence of misunderstandings and heartaches; which condition of things may continue for many years, for the patience and tenacity of the sign show in this as in all other matters, and a misplaced affection, even if apparently conquered for a time, will recur and reassert itself in spite of everything that reason and common-sense and worldly wisdom may say against it. When such a love as this – strong and lasting – is based on real sympathy and understanding, and is triumphant in the end, the happiness attained is as intense as the previous suffering was severe; for where feeling is concerned this type knows no half-measures, and its love, which, as has been said, has much of the maternal element in it, is characterised by a great yearning to give, while asking for little or nothing in return. (1911:7)

We see, then, that it is almost impossible to write a nutshell protrait of the Cancerian, for besides admitting that he will be extremely sensitive and maternal, there is almost nothing else one may say, short of indicating that he will be very different from everyone else:

This sign is called the paradox of the twelve. A few harmonious people are to be found in it who, as far as known, have not given any especial attention to mental or spiritual development; but, generally speaking, the genius of the Cancer sign is exceedingly difficult to explain. Those born under it have a persistent will, a clutch of determination, intuition, and purpose. (1894:8)

So we see that Cancer is the 'paradox of the twelve', and with the 'persistent will, a clutch of determination, intuition and purpose', we are far removed from the original damning words 'timid, and dull'. It is of no use exhorting the Cancerians of the world to unite against this calumny: for whatever is said, and no matter how they are exhorted, we may be sure that they will remain ever sensitive and ever different!

83. *Reds, oranges, and warm colours are beloved by Leos.*

84. *The journalist W. T. Stead, whose Sun was in Cancer on Sirius.*

85. *The 'Titanic' disaster, in which Stead lost his life. Fixed stars often lift up to eminence, and then drop the native in a most dramatic way.*

86. *Endymion, who symbolizes humanity, is kept in a trance by Silene, the Moon, who is in love with him.*

86

*87. Leo the Lion, in the fixed stars.
(From Bevis).*

*88. Leo loves to have an audience, if only
in his own mind. He likes to be
waited upon, or to be comfortable.*

*89. The Sun, the ruler of kings,
sovereigns, creativity and devotion.*

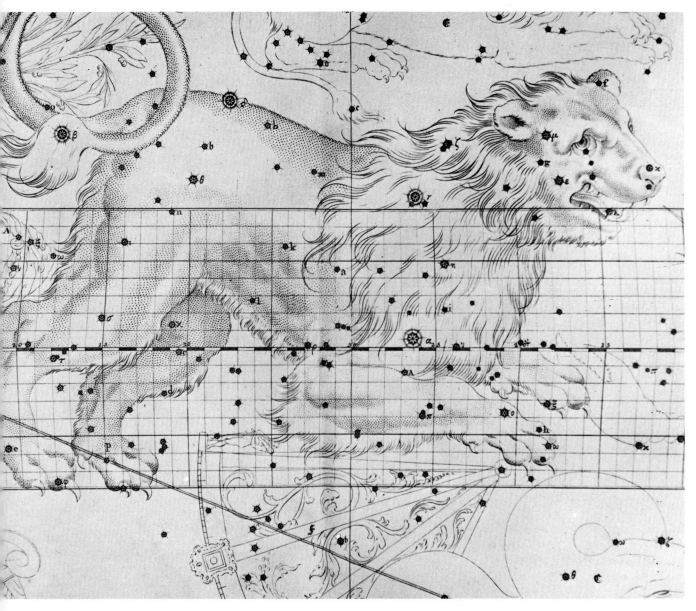

87

LEO

88

89

Sun in Leo gives a strong, well-made person; of a sanguine complexion; light-brown or yellow hair: full round face and large eyes; honest and upright in conduct, ambitious, and fond of pleasure. (1879:*1*)

Fond of pleasure the Leo type certainly is, often to his own loss, but this nineteenth-century miniature in no way does justice to Leo, for by modern standards he is essentially creative; the most obviously artistic of the twelve zodiacal types. No modern account of Leo could afford to miss out the creative strain in the type, as does the nineteenth-century description. A textbook miniature of an earlier date is more flattering, yet again it does not touch upon the important creativity of Leo:

Leo...denotes that the native will be of a large masculine body, broad shoulders, and austere countenance; dark or yellowish hair, large commanding eye, sprightly look, and strong voice; the visage oval, ruddy, or sanguine; a resolute and courageous spirit, aspiring mind, free and generous heart, with an open, bold, and courteous, disposition. (1795:*2*)

So it seems that we are faced with a very real problem: is the sign Leo, which is nowadays linked with all artistic enterprises, from painting and music to writing and the theatre, really creative at all? Curiously enough, few descriptions before the nineteenth century link Leo directly with artistic activities, even though Italy, the home of Renaissance art, was and is ruled by Leo, and even though there can be little doubt that the sign Leo has provided the world with many great artists in all centuries (figure 92). Perhaps the reason for this important omission may be found in the

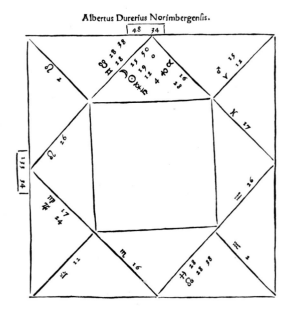

Albertus Durerius Norimbergenlis.

90

91

92

fact that the Sun has sole rulership over Leo,
and in the past it was always taken for granted
that even the layman would know that Leo
was ruled by the Sun. When an eighteenth-
century astrologer said 'Leo is the only house
of the Sun...' then it may have been intended to
imply that Leo was *therefore* creative, for after
all, was not the Sun the source of all life? The
Sun was not a round disk of fire in the sky,
somewhat like a guinea',* but a hole in the
fabric of the sky, through which men might
look into eternity. The Sun was more than 'an
immense globe or body of fire' to most men, for
when it was strongly placed in a horoscope, as
for example when it was in its own sign Leo,
then it made the native:

> ...kind hearted, generous, sympatic, and
> magnetic... They are emotional, very in-
> tuitive, and are generally able by means of
> this power to escape the consequences of their
> actions... When the true individuality of Leo
> holds sway, these people have a noble ideal,
> with a loyal love, confident, pure, and
> abundant. Having minds of the practical,
> philosophical, and spiritual combined – a
> triunity – they radiate a luminous substance,
> which makes them a most powerful people for
> good, with a marked ability to inspire others.
> (1894:*3*)

In other words they are noble, magnanimous
generous, and humane – the very image of a
king, and a description good for the ego of any
Leo type, yet again one observes the absence of
that word *creative*. The best modern short
description of Leo also fails to mention creativity in its usual sense of artistic creativity,
though it does mention that the occupations of
Leo include

> organists and musicians showing preference
> for the really grand and inspiring in their art;
> artists, actors. (1917:*4*)

yet significantly the earlier notes on the
personality of the type touch upon the creative
outlook of the type:

> ...none leave one so impressed by their
> sincerity as do the Leo types. They are
> generous and warm-hearted, cheerful and
> sociable, and there is a sterling worth about
> most of them which cannot pass long

* *William Blake. Descriptive Catalogue, 1810. Blake
had Mars in Leo, but what is more relevant to the
quotation is that he had Leo on his second house, which
of course governs money!*

90. '*The Rape of the Sabine Women*' by
the Leonine painter Rubens (*National
Gallery, London*). *The lively
composition, full, fleshy forms, and
theatrical setting are typically Leo.*
91. *Horoscope of the painter Durer.*
92. *Detail of a self portrait of Durer,
who looks typically Leonine.*
93. *The Sun driving the chariot of the
four seasons, with which he rules the
mortal world.*

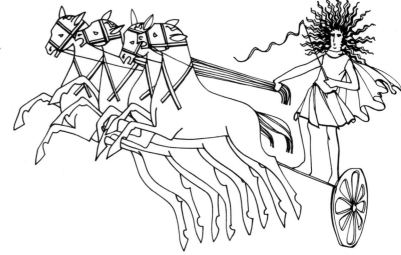

93

94. *The Leonine writer George Bernard Shaw. The very wide stride is typical of Leo – usually the type walks with great dignity and graceful bearing.*

95. *Alan Leo, the astrologer, set in the middle of his own horoscope which is strongly Leo. Leo types are often interested in astrology – especially those with 25° to 29° of Leo strongly marked.*

96. *Napoleon, the Leo 'King of Europe'.*

94

unnoticed. They rarely go totally to the bad, though many have to pass through the Fire of uncontrolled desire before they realise the Divine Spark within them; for the strength, vitality, and intensity of Leo when turned into sensual and dissolute channels is a terrible force, such a torrent as only Leo himself can stem. But the fall of Leo is more often due to the influence of others than inherent vice. Leo people are particularly subject to disillusionments with regards to their friends. (1917:5)

The 'Divine Spark within them' is, of course, the Sun in Leo, and the realizing of this divine spark may not always be the occupation of a saint – it may be done by everyman, and in his own terms. Leo usually realizes the divine spark within by using his radiating heat, the microcosm within him of the microcosmic sun, to warm those around him, to radiate his energy through his actions, through his sayings and through his works of art. The old tradition always emphasises the ambition of Leo, his energy, his urge to succeed, as well as the fact that he usually does succeed:

He that is born under the Sun, and he Royally dignified, is altogether aiming at Soveraignty, Rule and Dominion; and (according to capability) will be very famous... (1679:6)

His source of energy is immense, yet he gives it out freely, radiating it into whatever activity he decided to express himself through, be he an artist or a business man. The secret behind the creativity and success of Leo rests in the vast store of energy at his disposal, and in the fact that he will give this energy freely. The old woodcuts of Sol show him dispensing favours, radiating warmth in the very image of the Sun – perhaps this is why the starfish is ruled by Leo, for its undulating arms resemble the old drawings of a radiating sun. No wonder that he also rules the mythical phoenix, that strange Arabian bird which may be taken as a prototype of creativity. The Leo phoenix gives his all – burns himself to ashes, so to speak – yet comes forth with new life. It is not surprising that such a generous fount of energy would always be surrounded by people, an audience, and perhaps this is one reason why the Leo type always gives the impression of being something

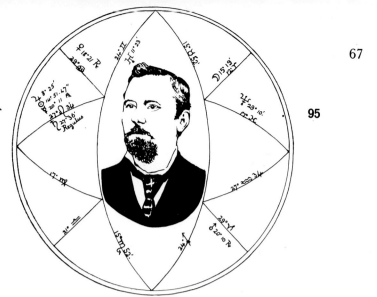

95

of an actor or actress – though, of course, one of sincere heart. He will believe in the part he plays. Any source of energy which gives out freely must be described as creative, and the significant thing about Leo creativity is that it happens almost automatically, even easily, for the type is an artist by nature. Other types in the zodiacal gallery must *work* at being artists. Leos take it for granted that they are artists, and their supreme confidence usually wins through:

> Under such conditions they have the most remarkable power in moulding public opinion, and in swaying great audiences. In fact, the truly awalkened Leo men and women are invincible if they will learn the pathway of silence. (1894:*7*)

But of course Leo is more than merely creative in the artistic sense – he is creative in whatever he decides to do. Let the astrologer Alan Leo, who, needless to say, was very much a Leo, comment on this:

> The Sun is in LEO. This gives you ambition, aspiration, ardour, and determination. You possess good organising ability; can manage and direct other people; are fitted for being at the head of affairs; and able to assume authority and command. If you exercise self-control you may achieve much success through strength of will and personal magnetism, and you will find you have much advantage over other people in these respects. You have much sense of personal dignity, but you are warm-hearted, good-natured, sociable, generous and magnanimous. This position is likely to lead you into some more or less responsible or prominent positions where you will have to direct or employ others, and you are likely to have success therein. Your feelings and desires are ardent, you have a strong sense of the dramatic, and a love of beauty and luxury. It is difficult for you to subordinate yourself to others or to occupy any position of inferiority, as you are a natural leader. (1910:*8*)

A very *constructive* type, indeed, and at his best in a position of authority. At a later point the same astrologer confesses his own weaknesses and points to the faults of our type, in a line

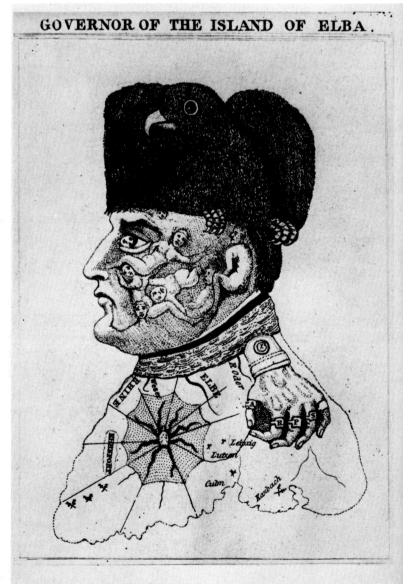

GOVERNOR OF THE ISLAND OF ELBA.

96

68

97. *The poet Alfred Lord Tennyson, who
    had the Sun in Leo. Leo men often
    wear beards.*
98. *The horoscope of Tennyson.*
99. *The horoscope of Mozart, to show
    the fifth house, which is the house of
    Leo, and which governs creativity, as
    well as children, the sex drive, and
    artistic products. The dividing line,
    marked with 14 degrees of Capricorn,
    is the centre of the house.*

100. *Aphrodite and Pan playing at dice.
    The fifth house governs 'chance', and
    all matters which appear to be the
    result of 'luck'. Gaming was in
    ancient times associated with
    divination: one put oneself in the hands
    of the gods, either to gain something or
    to learn about the future. The act of
    'putting oneself in the hands of the
    gods' is a fifth house matter.*

97

98

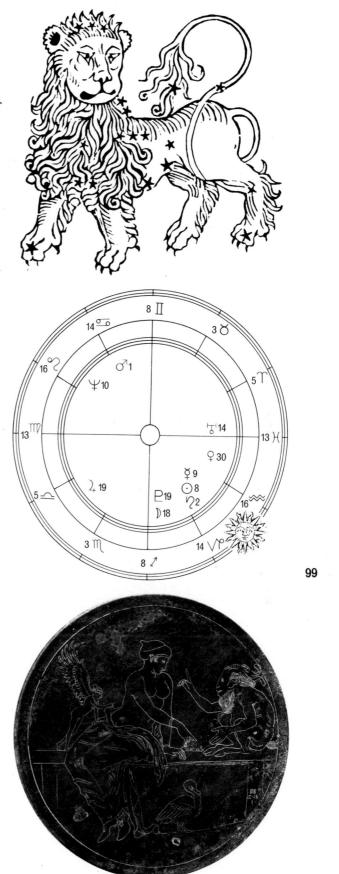

almost casually hidden between a string of ego-boosting epithets:

You will be internally generous, sincere, earnest, persevering and much inclined to self-perfection. This sign will give you affection, unselfishness, ambition, pride and love of power. Its dangers are cowardice, prevarication, love of pomp and show and a hasty temper. You are a lover of justice, also of the natural pleasures of life, but should avoid all excess of feeling and emotion. (1910:9)

Actually for once we must disagree in certain respects with Alan Leo – our type is rarely cowardly and he will usually react particularly well in emergencies: we recall that even in the eighteenth century it was recognised that courage was a Leonine trait, being of 'a resolute and courageous spirit'. One feels also that it is unfair of Alan Leo to advise his zodiacal kin to 'avoid all excess of feeling and emotion'. Leo was a Victorian after all and we suspect that the late Victorian respect for the stiff upper lip is out of place nowadays, particularly with the irrepressible Leo type. On the whole Leos should be left to feel and emote as they wish – and we may be sure that this will be to excess! The pleasure principle when repressed can turn quite nasty and a nasty Leo is a particularly unbearable piece of work. Leo rules the fifth house in a horoscope (figure 99), the house of pleasure, and perhaps this accounts for the fact that Leos usually have unsuccessful marriages at worst, traumatic marriages at best. Perhaps Leos should not marry, because marriage is an affair of the Libran seventh house which demands an ability to relate harmoniously with another person. The Leo is generally a shade too egocentric, too wildly committed to self, to cope in this delicate matter of relationship. The best advice is for the Leo to remain in the pleasure house but advice is rarely taken and most Leos marry twice. But is this a fault? Perhaps life is meant to be a matter of learning from experience, and in this Leo excels.

The faults of these people are most marked. Many of them are cunning, tricky, natural prevaricators, and chronic borrowers. They

99

100

101. The zodiacal man has the Sun to his right, the Moon to his left, as in some crucifixion pictures (plate 210). The Sun is lighting up the wrong side of the Moon, whose crescent should point towards the light. This symbolizes the tension in man between conscious aim (Sun) and subconscious (Moon). Man was meant to be a conscious monarchy, but is governed internally by a multitude (the Moon).

are hot-headed, impetuous, fiery, and passionate. They are easily attracted by the opposite sex, and are not usually distinguished for constancy. They take quick prejudices, but are sometimes more correct in their estimate of people than their cooler-headed and more passive neighbours. There are occasional liars to be found in this sign, and like the cat some of them will appropriate that which is not given them. (1894:*10*)

The faults of the sign are in fact more directly linked with *excess* than with any actual repression, for 'The sun in the ascendant, makes eminent Boasters and very proud persons'* as a seventeenth-century aphorism tersely maintains. At greater length we may see the same charge of excess, the same description of the Sun in his chariot being carried away by too many horses (figure 93), in a nineteenth-century account:

Primitive Leonians are generally afflicted with an unquenchable thirst for personal glory, and a ridiculous ambition for positions of responsibility and authority, which they are quite incapable of filling with any degree of success. Many, especially those of the commanding, or masculine type, contrive to give themselves the illusion of kingship by assuming airs of self-importance and lording it over their inferiors and juniors. The gentler or more feminine type seeks, above all things, a comfortable throne – and a well-cushioned one at that; and asserts her queenship by betraying a marvellous skill in delegating disagreeable duties, a total incapacity for serving either herself or anyone else, together with a wondrous power of swallowing flattery.

The Lion seen through a diminishing glass is very much like the domestic cat — an animal attached to its home and, as far as in it lies, to those who are willing to stroke it the right way; but never much inclined to put itself out for anybody. Even at his best and grandest the King of Beasts is no warrior; and indeed some naturalists have stigmatised him as the greatest fraud that ever wore a crown. He attacks his prey from behind, selects the weakest antagonists, and strikes them at their most unguarded moments. It is good generalship — the wiliest of warfare; and when the arm extended to strike is no arm, but an army, and the object of all this manoeuvering is the saving of bloodshed and the speedy conclusion of hostilities, the method is kingly though hardly heroic; but the monkey who makes use of the cat's paw to save his own skin shows the same tendency at a more elementary stage, and nobody finds his example inspiring. A talent for deputing work is first cousin to the habit of shirking it; and it behoves every son of Apollo to ask himself candidly where he draws the line. The pitiable state of muddle found in some Leonian kingdoms is due to the fact that the monarch has claimed the throne too soon, and is either inclined to fidget in it or to snooze...

The vice of kings is favouritism; and exaggerated faith in humanity may lead to many a blunder in the choice of friends. Primitive Leonians are apt to select those who can make themselves useful, or who flatter them by showing a certain amount of abject dependence on their favour. Their love affairs develop along the same lines, and are apt to be numerous and unfortunate. (1911:*11*)

We may round off Leo on this rather harsh note, confident that the Leo reader will not have had his own ego easily disturbed, for he will certainly not recognise in the above portrait any fraction of himself. Leo has a love for himself and if it is a greater love for self than with the other zodiacal types, it is generally a healthy one. His redeeming feature is that he also loves the world. The Sun also loves the world, and though we sometimes complain of his heat, let him be gone, and we go too!

* *John Gadbury's twelfth aphorism. A Century of Aphorisms. J. Partridge. 1679.*

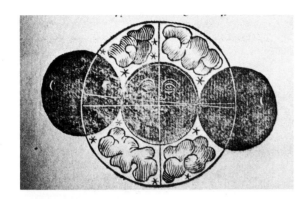

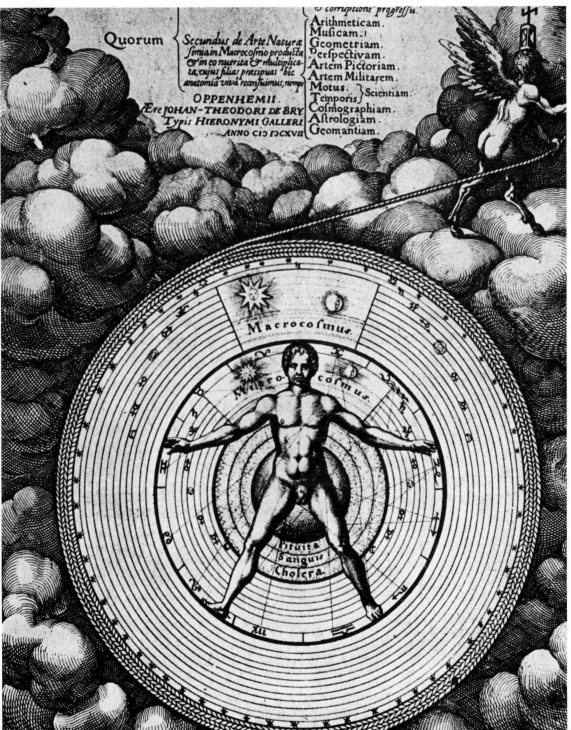

102. *Virgo the maiden, in the fixed stars.* (*From* Bevis).
103. *Virgo as the young girl.*
104. *The Virgoan likes to put all its attention into minutiae.*
105. *Mercury, the god of communication, riding in his chariot. It has been suggested by many astrologers that Mercury is not really the ruler of Virgo, as his nature finds little adequate expression through the sign.*

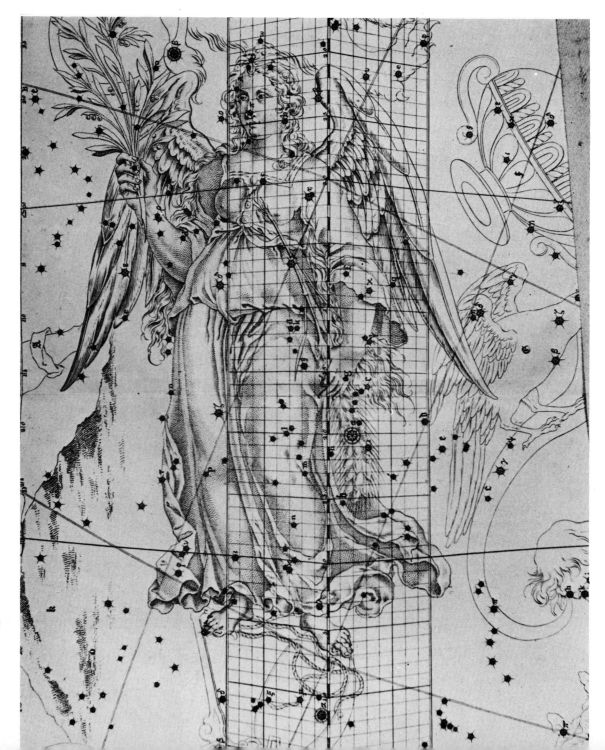

102

VIRGO

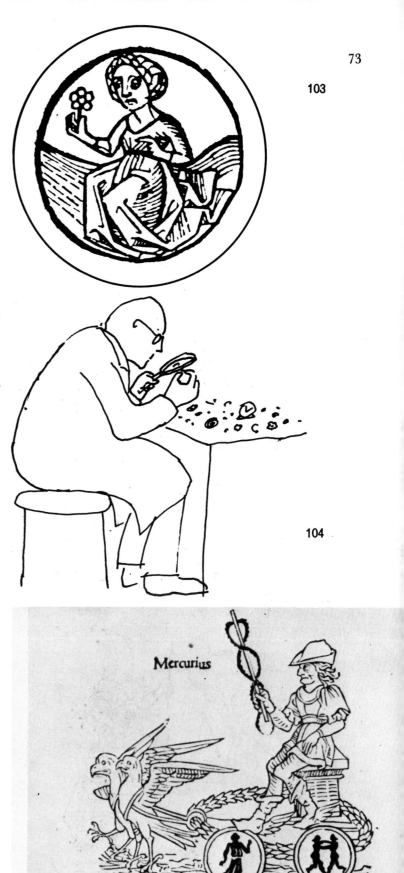

104

Mercurius

105

Virgo...describes a person somewhat tall and slender, well-composed; the hair very black or very brown; the visage more oval than round, all parts inclined to brevity, it shows a wicked, discreet excellent well-spoken person, very studious and given to all matters of Learning. (1679:*1*)

One would scarcely take this to be a description of the young girl, the *virgin* or maiden derived from the Latin name *Virgo*. The original Virgo was a pretty girl, sometimes with the wings which survived into late mediaeval images (figure 115), but by the time of Partridge quoted above, the wings have obviously been cropped, and she has become studious and 'given to all matters of Learning'. Clearly, even by the seventeenth century the astrologers have become worried about the rulership of the quick-witted Mercury over Virgo, for the volatile god of communication, whose character may be seen in Gemini, appears to have little to do with the reputation attached to Virgo. Indeed, by the end of the last century astrologers were suggesting a hypothetical planet Vulcan as ruler, mainly in order to give back to Virgo her youth, her charm and her wings. These historical generalisations are unfortunately necessary because the Virgo type is one of the most maligned of the zodiacal tribe: the 'old maid' virgin has in popular lore wrongly usurped the position of the youthful attractive maiden. Yet the heartening thing is that any practising astrologer knows that many Virgoans are more than merely 'witty, discreet excellent, and well spoken' – they are often lovely in a very delicate way, and almost always charming. Even the early astrologers – at least, those who

106. A nude drawing by the Virgoan artist Ingres. Like most Virgoans, Ingres was a perfectionist in both composition and colour sense. He used meticulous wrought detail in his paintings.

107. The Virgoan loves literature, and is well-known for its sharp critical sense. Virgo 'signifies a Study where Books are...' (Lilly)

108. The 'Virgin' Queen Elizabeth I.

106

worked practically rather than from books – were aware of this:

A slender body of meane height, but decently composed; a ruddy browne-complexion, blacke hayre, well-favoured or lovely, but no beautiful creature, a small shrill voice, all members inclining to brevity; a witty discreet soul, judicious and excellently well spoken, studious and given to History, whether Man or Woman; it produceth a rare understanding... (1647:*2*)

It is hard to understand why the 'well-favoured or lovely' may also be not beautiful, and we can only appreciate this in terms of the confusion which has occurred as a result of the old maid taking over from the young girl. But let us leave the appearance of our subject, noting the while that there is so strong a streak of femininity in the type that even Virgoan men appear to be slightly effeminate – they *appear* to be effeminate in some way, but they rarely *are* effeminate in fact. Let us study the temperament of our type, a temperament which appears to have been as little understood as the appearance:

Sun in Virgo describes a tall person slender and comely; plentiful hair of a brown, mind ingenious artistic and scientific; disposition cheerful and agreeable. (1879:*3*)

All astrologers agree that she has a good mind – for does not Virgo rule 'within doors, a Closet Study where Books, Writing are laid',* and is not the well-disposed Mercury significator of:

Men of admirable sharp fancies, extremely studious and capable of learning, guilefull or wily, wise, wary, divining well, or giving good advice, acting all things with agility and dexterity. Poets, Geometricians, Mathematicians, Astrologians, Eloquent, learning any Art, of good carriage or deportment. (1651:*4*)

The good mind and ingenious is admitted, though it is less commonly agreed among astrologers that the disposition is cheerful and agreeable. The truth is that Virgo has a reputation for being critical and carping, and indeed the faults of the sign are usually described in terms of an excess of negative criticism. Virgo is pre-eminently a sign of criticism and discrimination, especially as regards details, and the commonest failings of the Sign are the

* *Partridge Astrological Vade Mecum* 1679.

outcome of this tendency. They may be chronic fault finders, cantankerous, prejudiced, and narrow in their views, with the result that they are unpopular with those who misunderstand their natures. (1925:5)

So let us be fair, and attempt to understand their private inner world. In fact it is true to say that the major faults of the Virgoan spring from an inability to make decisions (which is an integral part of the Mercurian nature), and a tendency to be swamped by detail, as this rather uncompromising though humorous description of the modern Virgoan faults reveals:

The Virgo type is, before all else, short sighted, when the house is on fire Virgo, on the way to the phone, will see a pin on the floor and go in search of a suitable box to put it in. Arriving in paradise, Virgo would complain that the singing was too loud and slightly off key. The male Virgo is incapable of driving in a nail for lack of the ideal perfectly designed hammer. (1964:6)

If we examine the faults of our type in the light of nineteenth-century astrology, we have a kinder and more sensitive understanding of the virtues which reside behind the faults:

They are generous, and very solicitous about other people's affairs. They are usually much interested in the love matters of their friends, and have little hesitation in making or breaking matches. They are fine scholars, and make inspirational musicians. They keep their own secrets, and guard the secrets of their friends with equal fidelity. They are capable and efficient in all they undertake, being excellent planners and designers. The women are particularly fastitidious about their dress, and like to lead the fashion. They are affectional and devoted in the family, and are strong believers in blue blood. They aspire to the best things, but they are easily discouraged in their climbing. These people are natural philosophers, and possess the most accurate intellectual discrimination of the whole twelve signs of the Zodiac. They are capable of reaching great heights as writers, public speakers, and musicians; they are natural chemists, and often excel as newspaper editors. (1894:7)

107

108

109. *Vulcan at work. Some astrologers have suggested that this constructive god would make a more appropriate ruler over Virgo, for he is essentially practical, and works for others in a skilled profession. As one astrologer puts it 'His glowing furnace tries and tests and purifies the materials at his disposal separating the true metal from the dross'. (Pagan)*

109

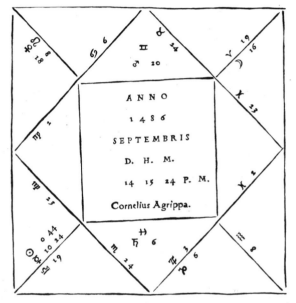

110

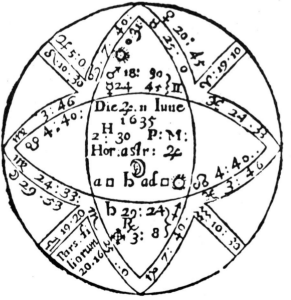

11

The fact is that the Virgoan is often so retiring that she presents a mask which is slightly unpleasant in order to protect a highly sensitive interior:

It may be said they maintain their cool and dignified attitude and often impressive presence at the expense of an ill-deserved reputation for coldness of feeling; and thus their nature is rarely, if ever, seen. (1917:8)

In other words, behind the mask of the stiff old maid there lurks a young girl who wishes not to be seen in her nakedness. Having noted this, let us see what the nineteenth-century astrologer has to say:

The average Virginian, instead of mastering detail, allows detail to master him, and if he takes up literature at all is more likely to succeed as a critic of other people's work than in any field demanding creative power. His style, though concise and clear, is somewhat formal, and best suited to the framing of business notices. He will draw up an index or a catalogue, compile a dictionary, or lend a hand in the production of an encyclopaedia. Hard work never daunts him, and to express himself with neatness and precision is a real joy; but apart from criticism his pen seldom runs freely, and his letters are usually the driest of the dry.

It has been neatly said, and the saying is often quoted, that the critics are those who have failed. It might be said with greater charity and fuller truth that the critics are those who are not yet sufficiently evolved to succeed; and of these critics, the most captious, and aggravating and impossible to please are the underdeveloped Virginians. The advanced type, bringing its clear vision and fine discrimination to bear upon the work entrusted to it, sees at a glance all the practical possibilities and opportunities for usefulness involved. The primitive type only sees the impossibilities and the flaws; and it finds them, by preference, in work done or schemes drawn up by others. The developed specimen never asks for praise; the primitive specimen never gives it. The former will conquer adverse circumstances, and make his very handicaps contribute to his success. The latter

110. *The horoscope of Agrippa, the magician, astrologer, and occultist.*

111. *A horoscope cast not for a moment of birth, but in order to determine a response to a question. The Virgoan Ascendant guides the astrologer in his attempt to say 'If the Querent should ever have children?' (From* Lilly*).*

112. *Goethe skating in Frankfurt. Goethe's horoscope which he cast himself shows both the Sun and Venus in Virgo.*

112

quarrels with every condition imposed upon him, resents his limitations, and invariably blames circumstances for his failures. His ambitions to achieve something practical and his inability to do so are apt to result in impatience, nervous irritability and ill-humour; and sometimes in chronic discontent. If hampered by ill-health or in any way restricted in his activities, he takes it cantankerously sometimes working on till deadbeat in defiance of the doctor, and meeting all the kindly remonstrances of his friends with a snap and a growl. Even at this rudimentary stage he has very little laziness about him, and if he is under wise guidance and control will make an admirable servant, loyal to his master's interests, and rigidly faithful to his orders; but these orders must be clear and precise, and the reversal of one of them, especially if sudden and unexpected, will upset the Virginian temper completely, and make him, for the time being, a very disagreeable companion. His horizon is bounded by the circle of his own duties, and by dint of concentrating his attention solely on the details immediately under his own nose, he loses sight of the larger outlines and consequently cannot adapt himself to changes which spring from causes beyond his ken. His views are not merely limited, they are microscopic, and he is apt to make mountains out of molehills on every possible occasion. He is the kind of man who is capable of surveying some Masterpiece of art in a stony silence that chills the blood of any real lover in his company, and who, before turning away, will point out mercilessly some trifling error in the darkest corner of the background, some tiny flaw in the construction of the frame. (1911:*9*) The general image is not so much of one who is evil, as of one who lacks self-confidence. So let us not peer too closely behind the mask, and let us consider more carefully some of the many virtues, a few of which are contained in the following nut-shell description:

Characteristics: good mental abilities, ingenious, active mind, apt at learning, sympathetic, quiet, retiring, methodical, critical. (1905:*10*)

Sympathetic and methodical, and with an active mind – what more can one want of any human being? In addition, because they are particularly sensitive to what things may be improved upon, it is true to say that even the 'fault-finding' for which they are famous is often basically creative and may be seen as a virtue, when looked at from a cosmic point of view. This is because behind their external criticism they are conscientious, reliable and consider themselves improvers:

There is a certain objective repose in Virgo-people which enables them to look leisurely at the work they have in hand and thereby take in the precise technical requirements of the same. Moreover, as their accent in life lies on the idea or nature of 'technical requirements' even the least fault, mistake, or error catches their attention; this makes them so critical and accurate. In Physics the 'critical temperature' means the point where a solution begins to crystallise out. So Virgo-people very often act in a similarly critical way in their surroundings, where their appearance may cause the recognition of long existing errors or awaken the consciousness to facts overlooked before, either in science, techniques, and traffic, or in morals. (1931:*11*)

We see then that the Virgoan should be considered more *discriminating* than critical. When the temperament of the type is understood properly – without reference to the misleading 'coldly-virginal' tradition – the type may be seen as a potentially creative young girl, perhaps rather modest and retiring, yet indeed, with that great saving grace in any human being – the ability to ask questions! Upon this ability rests the future of our race.

80

113

114

113. *The horoscope of Elizabeth I, who had Sun in Virgo.*
114. *The horoscope of Henry VIII, who had a Virgo Ascendant, with Mars in that sign.*
115. *Virgo, the pretty young maiden with angelic wings. From a mediaeval manuscript (British Museum).*
116. *'The Source' by the Virgoan painter Ingres (Louvre). The subject, the chastity of the subdued colours, and*

115

117

the economy of the simple composition
make it a typical Virgoan painting.

117. *Jerusalem, the centre of the mediaeval
world, is ruled by Virgo.*

118. *Paris is traditionally ruled by Virgo,
though a Leo rulership is more likely,
in modern times. Virgo also rules
Baghdad, Lyons, Padua and
Reading. Los Angeles is probably
ruled by this sign.*

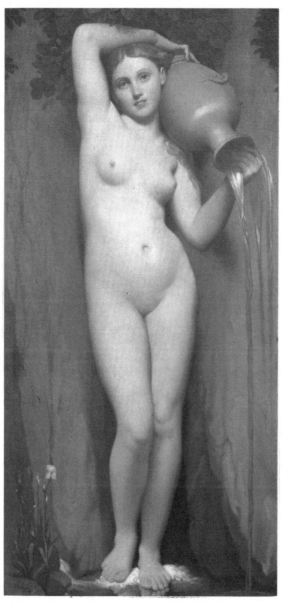

116

118

119. *Libra the Scales, in the fixed stars.*
120. *The Libran has a reputation for being lazy, and for delighting in gentle occupations.*
121. *Venus, the gentle ruler of Libra, in her chariot with Cupid, who is always involved with Libran activities.*

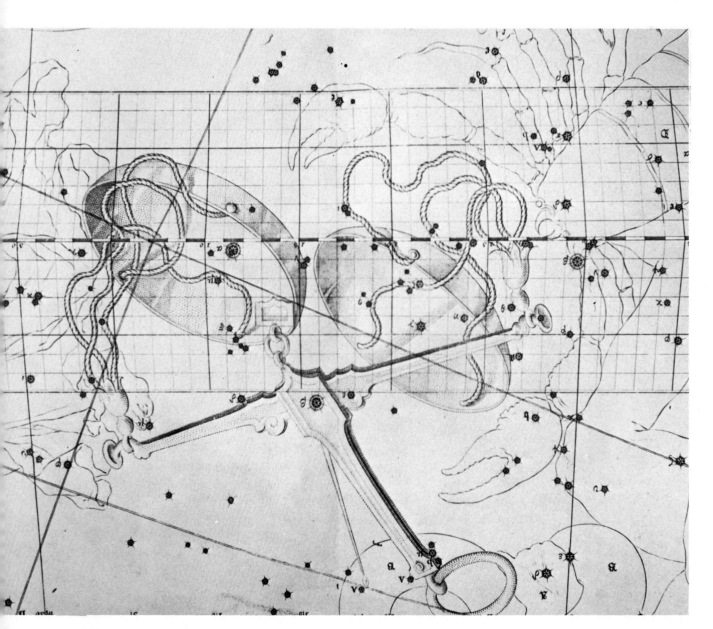

119

LIBRA

Libra...produces one of a tall, strait, and well-made, body; of a round, lovely, and beautiful, visage, a fine sanguine complexion in youth, but in old age commonly brings pimples, or a very deep red colour in the face; the hair yellow, or somewhat tending to flaxen, long and lank, grey eyes, of a courteous friendly disposition, with a mind just and upright in all his pursuits. (1795:*1*)

Taken all in all, this eighteenth-century quotation gives a fair, though superficial, idea of the Libran. Perhaps it is necessary to add a line from an earlier century to complete the picture: 'inclined rather to leaness than fatness',* though the type does tend to put on weight with advancing years. The Libran, both male and female, is generally beautiful in appearance, just and upright in disposition, and he does have a great sympathy for others, but of course, the account can scarcely end there. One of the most satisfactory descriptions come from the nineteenth century:

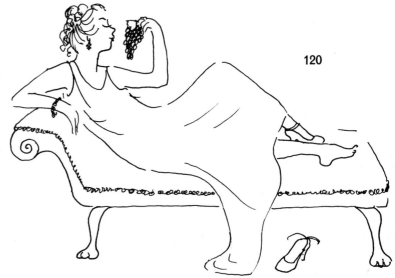

120

People born under this sign are energetic, ambitious, generous, and inspired. The men and women are said to differ even more than Leo men and women, and probably from the same reason. The Libra men having had to seek their own way, and to find their own companions and occupations, early learn to turn their inspirations and their clairvoyant ability to financial account, and so become stock-brokers and sometimes gamblers. The scales of Libra tip very easily, and too often one scale touches bottom with a dead weight, while the other swings aloft unused and empty. Libra men are very fascinating, and they are as reckless in following out the

Venus

* *J. Partridge. Astrological Vade Mecum. 1679. To give Partridge his due, he does continue :...'and round lovely beautiful Visage...'.*

122. *A view of Vienna, ruled by Libra, which also has rulership over Lisbon, Frankfurt, and possibly over Chicago and Miami. Libra rules Argentina, China, Egypt, Japan and Tibet.*

123. *The horoscope of the composer Liszt, who had the Sun and Mercury in Libra.*

122

123

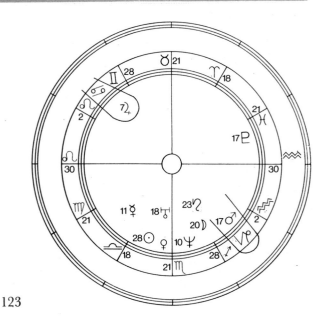

gratification of their desires as they are in gambling games and speculations. This pursuit is not so much sensual as sensuous, and is more of an eagerness for new objects of attraction than an impulse of passion. When over-taken by disaster, they recover quickly and go to work again with redoubled vigour. Their feet never touch the earth in their calculations and intrigues. They are full of hope and enthusiasm, and crash after crash produces no effect. The Libra women who have not had the masculine liberty are not so reckless as their brothers. They are apt to be careless about money matters, and this is often due to their extreme aversion to the financial part of any transaction. They detest being mixed up with money matters. They are not intentionally dishonest, for they always expect to be able to pay their debts, and often borrow with the noblest intentions, but if anything occurs to thwart their calculations – and ten to one it does – they expect the person borrowed from to be as magnanimous in forgoing the debt as they would be in paying it if they had the money. And yet these people, both men and women, have a keen and beautiful sense of justice; they are also exceedingly intuitive and mediumistic. When spiritualised, the scales hang evenly balanced, and the work that can be accomplished for humanity by the Libra people cannot be overestimated. Among them are poets, writers, and musicians. They soar high because the most rarefied air is their native element. They will give away the largest half of anything they possess, and never expect any equivalent. They are timid and apprehensive of disaster to their children and friends, and cause much nervous anxiety to their families and others...Libra women are very kind and amicable, and are averse to any cruelty and bloodshed. The women and children dislike to know that even a chicken must be killed. They are very neat, and dislike any hard and dirty work. The other type of Libra people is to be found more among the males who have broad round foreheads, and are cunning and quick speculators, having wonderful perceptive faculties. These will usually be found in the stock

124.

124. *The graceful Swan is ruled by Libra.
If the Venus of Taurus rules the
pigeon, then Libra certainly rules the
nightingale.*

125. *'La Gamme d'Amour' by the Libran
painter Watteau. The simple balance
of the composition, the pastel colours,
the subject of love and music, make
this a typically Libran painting.*

125

markets, where they are very fortunate. These men are apt to be very inconstant. (1894:*2*)

It is the rulership of Venus which makes the Libran so charming, artistic and refined, so much a lover of pleasure and of beauty. Fortunately, the Venus which creates so many difficulties with the Earth sign Taurus (see page 40), is more gentle in Air of Libra. This gentle Venus, when strong in a horoscope, gives:

Pleasant, chearfull and fair conditioned men or persons, decent in their apparell, good, bountiful, mercifull, prone to their delights, given to be cleanly, and to take the pleasure in sports and pastimes, subtill, elegant, poeticall. (1647:*3*)

the vision of Venus and her influence in the following century agrees in spirit, for she still denotes:

a handsome, well-formed, but not tall, stature; complexion fair and lovely, bright sparkling eyes of dark hazle or black, the face round, regular, smooth, and engaging; the hair light brown, hazle, or chestnut, shining and plentiful; the body regular and well-proportioned; and of a neat, smart, and airy, disposition; generally with dimples in the cheeks or chin, and often in both; the eye wandering, and naturally amorous; in motion light and nimble; in voice, soft ease, sweet, and agreeable, inclined to amorous conversation, and early engagements in love. (1795:*4*)

There is persistence in the beneficial influence of our ruling Venus, for in the following century another astrologer is still describing the characteristics of Libra in terms of charming qualities:

cheerful, genial, fond of company and amusements; good-natured, humane; affectionate, but changeable. Good mental abilities, but tending more in the direction of art, music, poetry, painting etc., than learning or scholarship; good powers of perception and observation. (1905:*5*)

The influence of Venus is therefore towards goodness and happiness: an astrologer of the eighteenth century, when called in to advise on a propitous time to begin a journey, would ensure that Venus was strong, for under its influence there would be 'much mirth pleasure, and success', as well as promise of safety and good fortune. This excess of good ointment must leave us wondering where the fly is to be found. What are the faults of the Librans? From the outset, we must echo the words of a nineteenth-century astrologer and admit that faults of the Libran are rarely serious ones:

the innate refinement of Libra must always be born in mind, as it gives a certain indefinable elegance and charm to all its children, making even the moral lapses which many a Libran fails to guard against far removed from the ordinary conception of vulgarity and vice. (1917:6)

Libran faults are innocent enough: the type is notoriously vacillating and almost always delays coming to conclusions until it is too late. They are also given to wanting a 'good time', enjoying themselves in matters of the body as well as matters of the spriit. Their curiosity also tends to lead them into 'faults', for they seek through their prying to draw conclusions whether these be founded on fact or not. They are subject also to the very human condition – be it virtue or vice – of jealousy. Admitting however that Librans have few actual vices, being wrapped in the cottonwool of Venus, let us look at their faults:

Libra people are apt to take things from a material, literal standpoint, and though their fine interior nature will often show them the true soul-side of the question, yet they often prefer and accept the conclusions of human logic. They are very impatient, and this causes them to lose much of their vital force, often bringing pains across the back. When they grow out of the lower desires, they make the most devoted and loving companions and parents.

These people are prodigal of their strength and talents, and scatter their forces in all directions. They feel it their imperative duty to help everybody, and seem to be utterly unaware of the fact that the ability to assist others is born of the power to govern self. It is exceedingly difficult for a Libra person to appreciate this truth. These are the people

126. *Wherever Venus is, Cupid will not be far away, for relationships and marriage are governed by Libra.* '*Venus, Mercury and Cupid*' *Correggio (National Gallery, London).*

127. *The Libran novelist Katherine Mansfield. Libran usually have high foreheads, and rarely cover them with hair.*

128. *Alphonse de Lamartine, the French poet, who is a typical male Libran.*

127

128

Each period of life is governed by a planetary cycle.

130. *The new-born child is governed by the Moon: "the infant mewling and puking in the nurse's arms." The child learns only by reflecting the manner and quality of those around it, in the same way as the Moon reflects the Sun.*

131. *The young boy, 'creeping like snail unwillingly to school' is governed by* *Mercury the God of communication. He is taught the values of society.*

132. *The period governed by Venus, 'the lover, sighing like furnace' the period of mating, the unwitting establishment of responsibilities. The move is towards the world in the form of another soul.*

133. *After marriage comes the period governed by Mars, when the energies are directed towards earning a living*

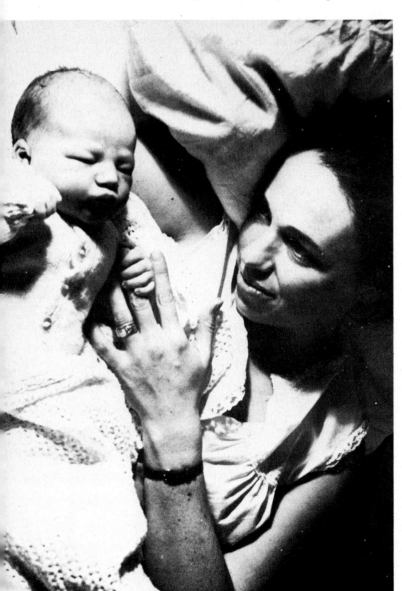

130

131

132

and for establishing a sense of separate individuality in life, through a career 'seeking the bubble of reputation even in the cannon's mouth'. Mars is always going somewhere doing something.

134. *The period of Jupiter, 'in fair round belly', the point at which the male reaches the zenith of his powers, surrounded by the welcome responsibilities of family life.*

135. *The period governed by Saturn. In present society this is usually a period of isolation, and the problem is one of loneliness, for Saturn is a planet of isolation, though it must be remembered that the planet also governs philosophy, and offers the possibility for finding the meaning of life by reviewing the lessions learned in the present incarnation.*
(As you like it – Act 2, Scene 7)

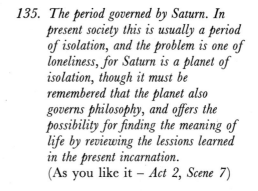

133

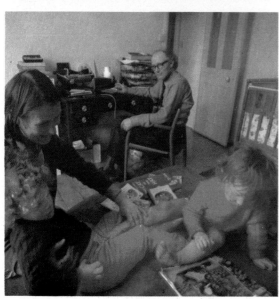

134

135

136. *The horoscope cast for the birth of Jesus Christ, which gives a Libran Ascendant. (From* Sibly).

137. *'Naked Woman Lying Down', by the Libran painter Boucher. A very 'lazy-Libran' subject, and Libran in composition...*

that are easily confused and confounded by the arguments of others, and who seem panic-stricken when lost in a crowd or compelled to cross busy streets. They are usually careless of their belongings, and are apt to drop and lose things. These are they who borrow books and do not always return them, and who are impatient of criticism on all subjects of omission or commission. They have an un-bounded desire for the approbation of others, and are foolishly wounded by trifles. They often seem more unreasonable and inconsist-ant than they really are, because of the work-ing of the sixth sense – intuition – which constantly aquaints them with the thoughts and feelings, states and conditions, of those about them.

Libra people are apt to espouse a new cause too readily, and often get into trouble through their enthusiasm, which seems never to diminish from the cradle to the grave. They are impatient of methods, and despise neces-sary routine. When angered, which is seldom, they leave nothing unsaid. The effect is like a cyclone, which leaves the air disturbed and cloudy for days afterwards. (1894:7)

As with the other planets, the earlier centuries tend to give a more lurid account of Venus and her influence,* but the following quotation sums up quite well the virtues and vices of Libra in terms of whether Venus is 'well-dignified' or 'ill-dignified' at the time of birth:

If well-dignified at the time of birth, the native will be of a quiet, even, and friendly, disposition, naturally inclined to neatness, loving mirth and cheerfulness, and delighting in music, amorous, and prone to venery,

though truly virtuous, if a woman; yet she will be given to jealousy, even without cause. If the planet be ill-dignified, then will the native be riotous, profligate, abandoned to evil company and lewd women, regardless of reputation of character; a frequenter of taverns, night-houses, and all places of ill-fame. (1795:8)

Fortunately, it is the cultivated Venus which clearly manifests itself in most Libran per-sonalities, the Venus which has rule over the arts, over pleasures and pastimes; significantly indeed over that musical centre of the world, Vienna (figure 122). It is the 'uncultivated' Venus which has rule over laziness, lust, the Venus which has indeed given us the very word *venereal!*

But it could be that we have concentrated for too long on the vices of a sign which is supposed to have few vices. We must redress the Libran balance once more, with a reference to a generous description containing no mention of vice, and which sums up the case for our sign exactly, as well as kindly:

Characteristics: cheerful, genial, fond of com-pany and amusements; good-natured, humane; affectionate, but changeable. Good mental abilities, but tending more in the direction of art, music, poetry, painting, etc., than learning or scholarship; good powers of perception and observation. (1905:9)

No evil here, no vices, save for a gentle hint at the traditional 'lazy Libra', the sluggards of the eighteenth-century zodiac, who prefer poetry to scholarship—but the Libran may take com-fort in the thought that this is no crime, except in the view of scholars!

* *See, for example, the influence of Venus on the sign Taurus (page 40).*

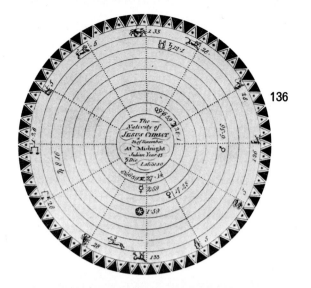

136

137

138. *Liverpool docks. Scorpio rules Liverpool, as well as shipping. The sign used to rule slavery, and in earlier centuries Liverpool was the main English port for slaves.*

139. *'Crying Woman'. A very Scorpionic subject, seen in a scorpionic manner, by a Scorpionic painter. The Scorpionic will pierce through reality, break it down into its compound parts, and then reassemble these in order to present a new image of reality. In this brilliant example, Picasso (who has Sun and Mercury in Scorpio) has succeeded in presenting the feeling of grief, through breaking down the conventional idea of grief. (Reproduced with the kind permission of Sir Roland Penrose).*

138

140. *Scorpio the Scorpion, in the fixed*
     stars.
141. *Scorpio rules the eighth house, which*
     is popularly called 'the house of
     death', It also rules spies, all strange
     situations, and hidden pressures. The
     ruler of Scorpio, Pluto, rules the
     underworld.
142. *Mars, the god of war, used to rule*
     Scorpio, until Pluto was discovered
     in 1930.

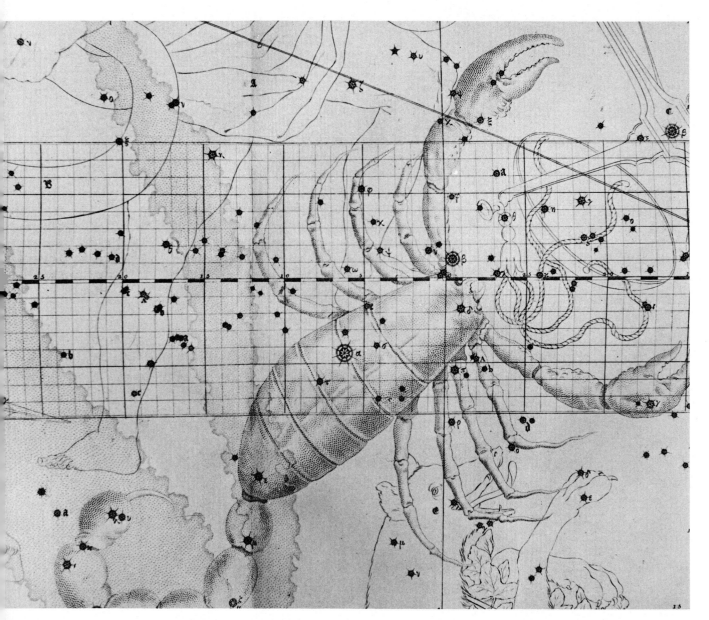

140

SCORPIO

. . . it gives a strong, robust, corpulent, body, of middle stature, broad visage, brown complexion, and brown curling hair; an hairy body, short neck, and short thick legs, quick in bodily motion, but reserved and thoughtful in conversation. (1795:*1*)

This eighteenth-century astrologer is careful to say precisely *nothing* about the temperament and disposition of Scorpio—one suspects because he is embarrassed by the fact that Scorpio has the worst reputation of the whole zodiacal herd. A century earlier, descriptions were less discreet:

Scorpio, an impudent fellow, a brazen face, yet of good understanding, covetous, arrogant. (1671:*2*)

The 'good understanding' is obviously a sop for the Scorpionic reader, but the general image is clear—Scorpio is something of a rotter! Another eighteenth-century quotation is also quite definite about this:

Scorpio has been found to afford to one class of human beings born when it is rising, a near approach in the expression of its countenance, especially in the eyes and the mouth to serpents; and when doing or saying cruel and bitter things, they are apt to be assimilated to the nature of snakes, scorpions etc. (1828:*3*)

Even in the enlightened nineteenth century the influence persists, for those born under Scorpio are still described as 'reserved, thoughtful, subtle, and malicious,'.* On the whole, therefore, one may understand why few people are proud to be Scorpionic when such epithets are flying around. In fact, there are good historical reasons why the sign should have such a bad image, but even in the seventeenth century one

141

Mars

142

* *The influence of the Stars*. Rosa Baughan. 1889.

astute astrologer was already urging Scorpionics to throw off the unfortunate reputation settled upon them:

It is high time for Scorpionists to awaken out of their lethargy, and look to themselves . . . let them rouse up for the Philistines are upon them in earnest. If (the . . .) black bill of indictment brought in against Scorpio were true, it is as great a crime for man or woman . . . to have Scorpio for their horoscope as it was for Dr. Lamb to be reputed a conjuror . . . It is argument enough for anyone to have Scorpio ascending at his birth to be predestined an heretick and an inhabitant in the kingdom of darkness after his death. (1675:4)

The astrologer was quite properly objecting to the many unfortunate epithets which the tradition attached to Scorpio, for these create a very villain indeed:

falsity, arrogance, ambition, ingratitude, boasting, lying, lechery, perjury, revenge, all manners of vice and lewdness . . . (1675:5)

Well, there is the tradition in all its stark severity, and an unfortunate tradition it is indeed, not only inaccurate and unfortunate but also hard to shrug off. In view of this, it is better that we sweep all these malicious words back into the past, and consider afresh what is the nature of the true Scorpionic. We may best do this by glancing at the nature of the planet Mars which used to have rule over Scorpio, until the discovery of Pluto, which is now the accepted ruler:

person of the type *Mars* are practical, fond of sport and war, courageous, confident, jealous of honour and in the affections; domineering but magnanimous, liberal; energetic, devoted to the opposite sex, wishful to enjoy life in unconventional society, and fond of brilliant surroundings. (1899:6)

Here we are nearer a true assessment of the Scorpionic type, for he is essentially practical, jealous of honour, tending to be domineering, but certainly magnanimous and given to the enjoyments of life. Two World Wars have tended to reduce anyone's fondness for war, and so nowadays the Scorpionic pours his rich aggressive energies in other directions. Energies which were once directed outwards are now contained within, with the result tha all Scorpionics are *intense*. This intensity enable the Scorpio to see through the superficia trappings of the world, with the consequenc that he frequently dispenses with the ordinar standards common to men. Being thus re moved from what is conventional he is fre quently rejected by those who prefer con ventionality, and frequently meets people whc fail to understand him. Perhaps this is why certain astrologers have conspired together to create such an unfortunate tradition. In the country of the blind the man who can see may have his eyes gouged out! Yet, in spite of this, by a curious inbuilt contradiction, we find that our type is thoroughly magnetic and attracts other people. And here, in particular, the Scorpionic intensity is called into play. Any relationship with the Scorpionic will be interesting, of this we may be sure—only too frequently the intensity is just too much, and it is best for the other person to just go away . . . However, let us look at an up-to-date description of the Scorpionic and note the virtues before we are carried away by the many faults:

. . . the Solar influence passing through this sign will make you a firm powerful character, arising from the silent force within, giving you also occult learnings. You possess magnetic power, critical perception and ability to judge keenly, but not when fully under control your character will be rather exacting, jealous and proud. You will have strong likes and dislikes, and can be very reserved and dignified, though when vexed you are apt to be sharp and sarcastic if not actually cruel. You will, however, have much self-control, determination, tenacity and secretiveness, and as life advances there will come a stronger desire to investigate the occult and mystical. Avoid pride, cultivate sympathy, and endeavour to see things from others' standpoints as well as your own. (1910:7)

The image is of someone living under the influence of an almost unbearable intensity, and the concluding plea is clearly intended to persuade the Scorpionic type that other people have an existence, as well as themselves. Most moralizing astrologers usually make a half-

143. *Pluto, the dark ruler of Scorpio, carrying off Proserpine to his underground domain. Scorpionic men often have a magnetic, hypnotic influence over women.*

144. *The horoscope of the astrologer John Gadbury, often quoted in this book. He has a Scorpionic Ascendant.*

145. *The Scorpio male. (From* Varley).

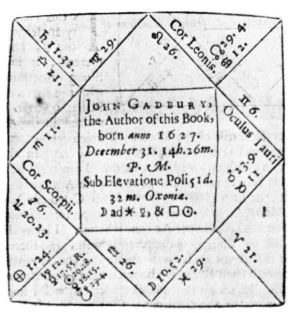

144

145

hearted attempt to eradicate something of the selfishness for which the sign is famous.

It could be that we have so far suggested that the Scorpionic cannot relate easily to other people, and whilst this is indeed one of the underlying problems, it is also true to say that the latent power in the Scorpionic permits the type to relate perfectly when it is a matter of leading or dominating. The Scorpionic can never take second place, and this may lead to difficulties. However, assuming that the Scorpionic is in the lead, then characteristics manifest a high powered personality:

So marked is this power that they are able to benefit all who are closely connected with them. Their personal presence is a healing. They possess indomitable will and self-control, and remarkable skill in the use of their hands. Their touch is so firm and delicate, their observations so keen, their poise so perfect, that they make the best surgeons in the world. They are not moved by the complaints or fears of their patients, and preserve the coolness of their native element under all circumstances, however trying. Such persons are often considered unfeeling and unsympathetic and this is sometimes true, though more frequently it is an appearance caused by a resolute and unflinching determination to succeed. Before an operation some of these surgeons are regarded by their patients as demons. Afterwards they are always gods.

The genius of eloquence is sometimes a direct inheritance of those born under this sign. They are powerful and magnetic public speakers, and when the spiritual nature is aroused they make the most popular and convincing clergymen. They have great tact and taste in the choice of language, and are usually very well aware of their influence over those with whom they come in contact. Those who write excel in the construction of short stories. One strong characteristic of these people is the silent, dignified superiority of appearance. This is a very important factor in their success. They are usually courteous and affable when not engaged in serious business; then they can be blunt to cruelty. (1894:8)

148. Mussolini, an example of a magnetic Scorpionic. Like all Scorpios, he had forceful, hypnotic eyes, of which he was very proud.
149. Edgar Allan Poe, the American poet story-writer who was like many Scorpionics interested in death, torture and the occult.

The image is that of the 'universal physician'— cool in delving into the causes of the particular illness of mind or body, and then coldly efficient in cutting away at the cause, to restore to health. The strange emotional detachment with which they do this makes lesser types suspicious of them, and for all their good intentions they often gain a reputation for being dishonest. This image is applicable to the Scorpionic on all levels of being, from that of personal relationships, where they have a reputation for a curious admixture of intensity and coldness, to business, in which their hard dealing often makes others regard them as untrustworthy. It usually takes another Scorpionic to best a Scorpionic in business. Perhaps this is why mediaeval astrologers considered Scorpio to be the sign ruling the Jews, for economic sanctions drove these people to the fringes of society—they being misunderstood, in the Scorpionic tradition—and compelled them to earn a living by the exercise of sharp wits and magnetism. Shakespeare's Shylock has been long held to be a figure of a Scorpionic! Fortunately, the image of Scorpio in the traditional lore is only distantly related to the Scorpionic we meet in real life today.

Perhaps we have been too nice to Scorpio. Perhaps we have gone too far in presenting an image of Scorpio which appears in glowing colours—the real colour of Scorpio is deep red, the colour of blood, as the tradition will hasten to add. Therefore perhaps we should finish with a brief glance at the faults which Scorpionics may truly be said to manifest:

Three great evils are apt to dominate Scorpio when on the animal plane. These are anger,

150. *The Russian novelist Dostoyevski. Crime and punishment is a common Scorpionic interest.*

151. *Mata-Hari, the famous female spy, who was born under Scorpio. The sign rules hidden things, and all those who penetrate into hidden matters in order to reveal – hence detectives and spies, as well as criminals (who work in the dark) are governed by Scorpio.*

148

149

150

151

100

*152. Admiral Nelson was Scorpionic.
Scorpio rules the navy and seamen,
mainly because it is a watery sign.*

*153. Sir Henry Irving, a good Scorpionic
actor, in the role of Mephistopheles.
The Devil and Hell is ruled by
Scorpio — the flames of hell being the
red favoured by Scorpionics, the
location being underground, as well
as the seat of spiritual agony.*

154. The horoscope of Irving.

152

jealousy, and passion, and, if permitted to hold sway, will destroy their integrity and ruin their lives. This sign is the natural propagative centre, and the unawakened Scorpio person is sometimes a monster of lust. The intense love of praise and flattery is another great weakness. The husband who does not coax and praise his Scorpio wife has not infrequently a very hard time of it. The education of the male has been different, therefore they are not always so exacting in small things, but when their suspicion and jealousy are fully aroused they want to kill, and sometimes do. The habit of procrastination and indolence are very marked, and if not broken become veritable diseases. Those who have not learned the higher law of love are often very unsatisfactory and eccentric in their dealings with their friends. A friend is a splendid fellow as long as he can be used, but when he no longer contributes to their happiness and well-being, he will be tossed aside with no more compunction than one would throw away a squeezed lemon. Later, if they feel that the assistance of the enemy is necessary, the bridge will be rebuilt and used to the utmost. Scorpio people have infinite tact in such matters, and their wonderful magnetic power enables them to destroy and restore these friendships with ease and grace. (1894:9)

But when Scorpio lives on a higher plane than the animal, then a great prince is born, with a great power to make and break other human beings at will. An ordinary Scorpionic is always strong and always the victim of passion —the remarkable Scorpionic is the one who has learned to control the passions, and deflect the resultant energies for the good of mankind. Scorpio rules the generative organs in man and it is therefore not surprising that, in the ancient diagrams, the generative organs are placed in the centre of the circle surrounding the zodiacal figure of the Cosmic man (figure 101). This stands as a symbol of the true and dignified Scorpionic, his wild energies contained and utilized for the purpose of creating other human beings in the image of God, in a word, for the purpose of regeneration.

153

154

155. *Sagittarius the Archer, in the fixed stars.*

156. *A completely human Archer. Normally Sagittarius is half horse.*

157. *The well-fed Sagittarian taking it easy, yet, as always, going somewhere.*

158. *Jupiter the ruler of Sagittarius, who governs sport, hawking, deep study and philosophy. The fishes at the foot of the god refer to Pisces, which Jupiter ruled in traditional astrology.*

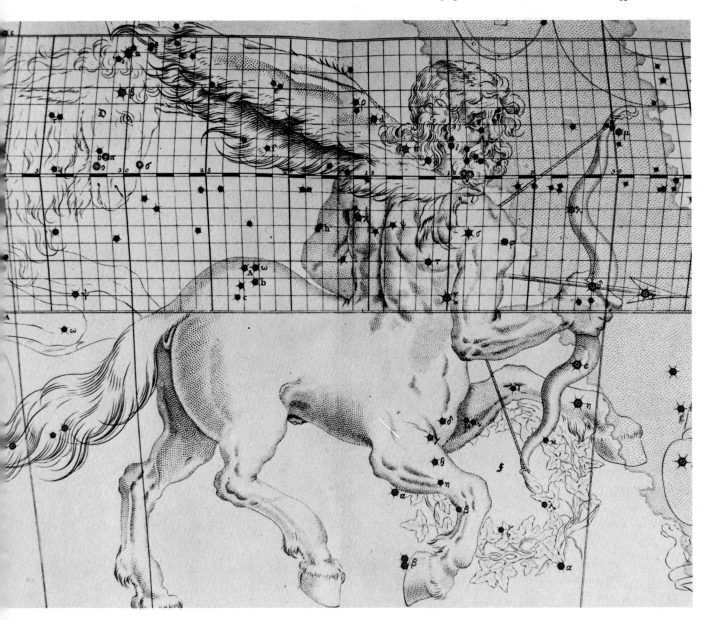

155

SAGITTARIUS

156

Sagittarius...endows the native with a well-formed body, rather above the middle stature; with an handsome, comely countenance, a visage somewhat long, ruddy complexion, chestnut-coloured hair, subject to baldness; the body strong, active, and generally makes a good horseman; stout-hearted, intrepid, and careless of danger. (1795:*1*)

Thus runs an eighteenth-century description of our sign, and if we substitute for 'good horseman', the modern equivalent 'fond of cars', and recall that the type loves *fast*, luxurious cars, we have a pretty good image of the modern Sagittarian, a portrait of the type who is quite justifiably the most popular in the zodiac. The Sagittarian has everything going for him, it seems, for he is ruled by the magnificent and expansive Jupiter, the Hebrew 'Star of Warmth', of whom the authority says:

157

> then is he Magnanimous, Faithfull, Bashful, Aspiring, in an honourable way at high matters, in all his actions a Lover of Fair Dealing, and desiring to benefit all men, doing Glorious things, Honorable, Religious, of sweet and affable Conversation, wonderfully indulgent to his Wife and Children, reverencing Aged men, a great Reliever of the Poore, full of Charity and Godliness, Liberll, hating all Sordid actions, Just, Wise, Prudent, Thankful, Virtuous... (1651:*2*)

Almost too good to be true, this Sagittarian, yet on the whole quite real in the way that the unicorn is real—for our fabulous Jupiter rules also over the fabulous unicorn; once you have met one, you will never quite forget. Besides the fabled unicorn, Jupiter rules over 'all domestic animals, that do not fly the dominion

158

159. *Sagittarius aiming upwards and outwards, as is his wont.*

160. *A horoscope cast by William Lilly to determine whether or not an escaped prisoner would be caught. The Sagittarian Ascendant, taken in relation to the Moon, implied that he would be caught.*

161. *The horoscope of Walt Disney, who had Sun and Uranus in Sagittarius.*

162. *Walt Disney and his creation Mickey.*

159

160

of man', yet the Sagittarian is not himself strongly domesticated. Perhaps he is only domesticated in the same way as the horse, which Jupiter rules also—happy to be in the stable at night, provided there are fresh pastures for the morning, and much exercise to satisfy his roving nature. The home for the Sagittarian is certainly a place to relax, a place which must be very comfortable, filled with beauty, even with music and good food, yet it is essentially a place from which one sets out, a point of departure into the large world outside, the proper aim of the Archer. He is a restless type, like the horse which is half of his nature (figure 159), yet his dignity prevents him from displaying his restlessness or his impatience, and this image has survived in its pristine form in a way that those of the lesser zodiacal types have not. We find even the modern astrologer describing him in rapturous tones:

Frank, honest, open, impetuous, good-natured, intuitive, sporting, strong sense of justice, irritable, generous, optimistic, independent, clever, versatile, quick, fond of prediction, fond of religious and philosophical subjects, fond of outdoor exercises, sport, and horses, apt to make shrewd shots and guesses, fond of giving advice. (1922:*3*)

This description of our unicorn is on the same level of ego-satisfying epithets as that offered by Ptolemy nearly two thousand years ago. In fact the seventeenth-century astrologer Lilly had difficulty in expressing the weaknesses and faults of the type, and in order to do so had recourse first to pointing out the virtues attached to Jupiter:

Honest, religious, just, liberall, magnanimous, Governours, eminent men, performing high matters, sober, grave with a kind of moderation, prudent, living virtuously and orderly. (1651:*4*)

This same Jupiter, when ill-dignified, gives us:

Lovers of themselves, open-hearted innocent; it declares manners much of the nature before recited, but more obscure and imperfect, a scornful, disdainfull, mind proud, superstitious, fearfull, dissembling, a kind of vain candour, negligent, prodigall. (1651:*5*)

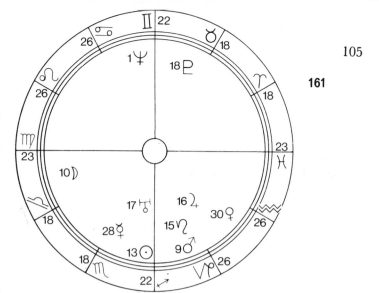

Few faults indeed, when they have to be described in terms of the virtues of the type. A nineteenth-century account, after admitting that Sagittarius 'rarely makes mistakes', dwells upon their faults at length:

People born in this sign have a tendency to fly all to pieces over a small matter, are quick to anger, but quickly over it, combative and determined to have their own way. As enemies Sagattarius people go to extremes. They may forgive and treat the one who has injured them with kindness, but they do not forget. They are unreasonable in their desire to help those they love, and zealous and over-sanguine in whatever they undertake. They are unwilling to wait for proper times and seasons, and desire to rush through every piece of work as soon as it presents itself. An unfinished task is an intolerable affliction; therefore Sagittarius people, especially the women, are likely to sacrifice health and good-nature in their determination to finish what they commence.

This alertness and incessant industry frequently causes trouble in the family. Those born under less active signs cannot see how it is possible for one to be forever busy. Sometimes these workers are very fond of their achievements and are exceedingly unhappy and disappointed if their efforts are not properly appreciated. The Sagittarius person who has had no training governing the faults of his sign, always aims in anger at the vulnerable spot of his enemy and is reasonably sure to hit it. Such a one when angered is very cruel.

These people expect too much of others. They are quick to observe, to plan and to do, and they make small allowance for those who are less gifted in such practical respects. Until they have learned self-control they are apt to be very exacting and domineering. (1894:6)

From the above it would seem that even with his faults, the Sagittarian is on the side of the angels. It is curious therefore that the author should actually presume to give advice to the type as to how he might achieve a higher spiritual growth:

They should cultivate calmness and repose, and think well and in silence before deciding

163

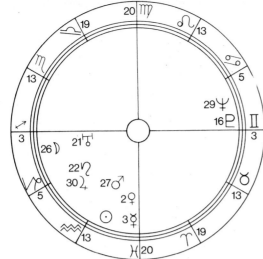

163. *The horoscope of the American aviator Lindbergh who is strongly Sagittarian.*
164. *Lindbergh in the cockpit of his flying machine, which along with the sports car is the modern equivalent of the traditional Sagittarian horse.*
165. *Jupiter holding the creative fire which he gave to mankind, and supported by the strong-winged eagle.*

164

an important question. They should not be governed by impulse in any charity work. They should strive to find their rewards for service in the unselfish motive which prompted it, and expect neither gratitude nor appreciation from any source but their own conscience...

The bluntness of Sagittarius people is cause of much unnecessary suffering to others, and they must not excuse themselves because of the truth of their words. They should learn to be gentle in speech and to give out the truth with discrimination. They should teach themselves not only to forgive but to forget ingratitude... These people should be very careful in marrying, as serious troubles are apt to occur from uncongenial unions... Their demand for purity and individuality in married life often causes great inharmony. These people are all very strong and loyal in their love relations, but when they are deceived or ill-treated it is apt to embitter their future happiness. The women become silent and hopeless, while the men are likely to indulge in drink or reckless despondency. (1894:7)

The advice is only vaguely applicable—perhaps *all* types should learn to be more gentle with other people, and certainly all types should be 'careful in marrying'. It would in any case appear to be a lost cause, this, to advise our Sagittarian to be calm and less impulsive, as the author does. The natural self control and dignity of the type often passes for calm, and their decisions are best made impulsively. If anything, the Sagittarian is *independent*; fortunately the advice given will be completely

Iupiter

166

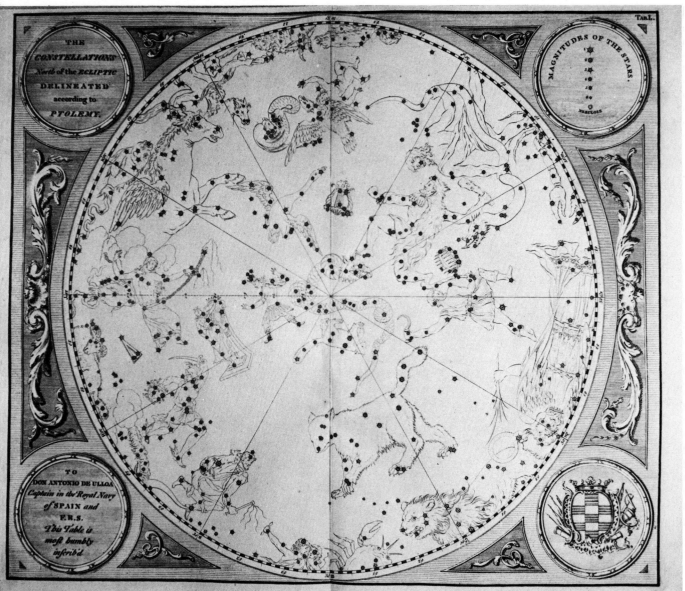

167

ignored, though it will no doubt be tended with the grave dignity and humour which characterises the Sagittarian manner. If there is anything more to be said about the so-called faults associated with Sagittarius, it is that these optimistic, cheerful, independent types are fond of other people, and delight in splendid company, in exhibiting their magnificent minds and magnificent beings—their 'faults' are manifested only when their independence is threatened or limited. But it could be that we have strayed too far into the darker side of one so much involved with light, as the Sagittarian undoubtedly is; and in so doing, we may have lost sight of the unicorn which so delights. Let us correct this tendency of ours:

Those belonging to Sagittarius are bold, zealous, determined and combative. Very quick to decide, act, and speak. Their mind is constantly running ahead. Going beyond the present, they have a tendency to peer into the future, and to forsee events. They hate anything hidden and secret, and even secret organisations. They go to extremes in everything they do, being overzealous and sanguine in what they undertake. As a friend, they are such with all their being; and as enemies they also go to extremes; their kind heart and loving, sympathetic nature, however, restrains them from acts of violence and evil deeds. They are high tempered, impulsive, and do things on impulse. They have great power over their sex natures, and have a natural inclination to chastity, and from this, as a prime cause, they have great physical power. They are physically the strongest persons of the whole twelve signs...

Some of the finest musicians come from this sign. They are faithfull in their love relations, and if they fail to get the objects of their choice, it usually embitters their entire future in life. They are domestic in their tendencies, sympathetic, devoted, and loving. They do not take opposition kindly, except a good reason be given. (1893:8)

Perhaps the above mentioned nineteenth-century account was inaccurate, even at the time; or perhaps the Sagittarian nature itself

166. *Jupiter in his chariot of state, with his eagles, being tended by a menial. When Jupiter is 'strong' in a chart (for example, on or near the Ascendant – see the horoscope opposite) it raises the native in society, and gives great power.*
167. *The constellations north of the ecliptic according to Ptolemy. The zodiac of astrologers does not correspond to the constellations of the astronomers.*

has changed in the past eighty-odd years, but certainly it is not true to say that the Sagittarian is the strongest of the zodiacal signs *because* he conserves his sex energies. This type conserves very little, in fact, and in the view of certain tiny minds one of his faults is prodigality, which in the realms of sexuality may express itself as profligacy. Jupiter is indeed temperate, but he is also noble-spirited:

Jupiter is temperate; the great social planet, bringing success, and governing all matters of a benefic nature. It represents the truly religious, and everything that is jovial, happy and free. It is the planet of benevolence, mercy, and compassion, and governs all those who are well-disposed, generous, loyal, and noble-spirited. It always represents superiors, moral and mental. (1905:9)

It is because of this that the Sagittarian needs freedom to expand, because he is by nature 'superior', and should therefore be in the lead. For this reason, also, Sagittarians are best adapted to work which gives liberty, opportunity for promoting and contact with other people. Hence the obvious connections with politics or the law, and even with the military: for this reason also advertising and public relations are ruled by Sagittarius. The truth is that the Sagittarian enjoys anything which is expansive—he enjoys life itself, and therefore it is not surprising that he should enjoy his sex life, along with the responsibility of his family life, provided that he is not too much tied down in place or time by petty emotional attitudes. In return for freedom, he will give freedom; and if he is not given freedom, then he will surely take it!

168. *Capricorn the Goat, in the fixed stars.*
169. *Capricorn the business man, standing awkwardly, suspiciously aware of his competitive neighbours.*
170. *Saturn the prototype of Father Time, with the destroying scythe, pulled by repellent dragons.*

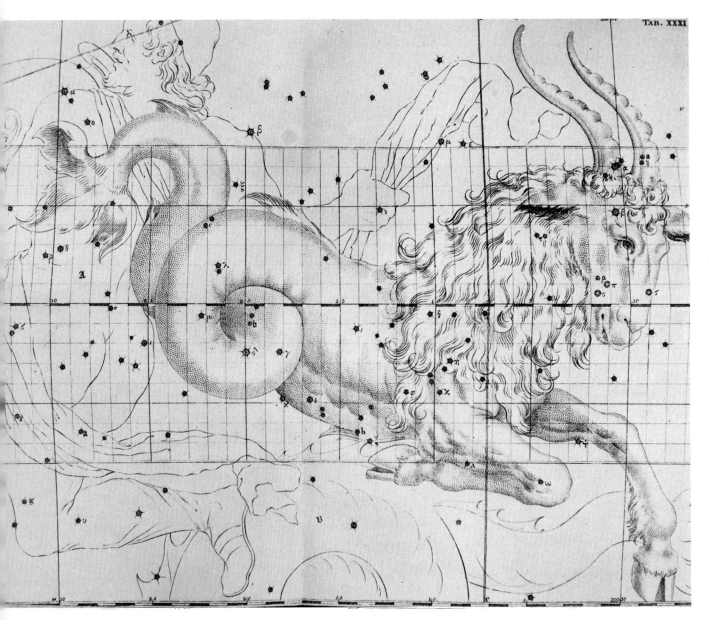

168

CAPRICORN

When this sign governs a nativity, it produces a slender stature, of a dry constitution, long thin visage, small beard, dark hair, long neck, narrow chin and breast; with a disposition that is collective, witty and subtle. (1795:*1*)

Capricorn's ruling planet, Saturn, governs the skeletal frame, that which is hidden inside the body, that which determines the outward form from within, yet inside the Capricornian is a being very different from his external appearance. The eighteenth-century astrologer quoted above stays mainly with the physical description of the type, affording only three words to the disposition, but, even in his 'collective, witty and subtle' there is a missing link. We need another word to pin down precisely the Capricornian temperament, a Saturnine word about which whole books have been written:*

CAPRICORN: Slender make, in some cases ill-formed or crooked; a long thin face, generally plain; thin beard; chin long and protruding; black lanky hair; narrow chest; disposition subtle, collected, calm, witty and yet melancholy. (1879:*2*)

And yet *melancholy!* Here, with this one word, we put the finger on Capricorn, for he is serious and austere in his appreciation of life, and this passes frequently for melancholy. The traditional image of the Capricornian is almost that of a melancholic goat, yet, to be fair to this maligned type, he should never have been a goat and originally was a goat-fish (figure 168). Although he is serious and often gives the impression of being melancholic, he has a delightful wit, and one suspects that he is melancholic only because he takes life so seriously—and of course he could be right, for

169

Saturnus

* For example, Saturn and Melancholy, by Klibansky, Panofsky and Saxl, 1964, or that splendid attempt to vanquish Saturn, The Anatomy of Melancholy, Robert Burton. 1621.

171. Saturn devouring his own son, emblematic of his role as the God of Time, who devours all things. Sometimes the Capricornian is his own worst enemy.

172. 'David' by Michaelangelo. (Accademia, Florence). The search for a perfect outer form is typically Capricornian.

171

life is a serious matter... The association with the goat has been linked in the past with sexual proclivities, and the result is that our Capricornian (in the past if not today) has a reputation he does not deserve:

Capricorn, portends a letcherous person, much given to the flesh, nor constant to his Wife or Mistress. (1671:*3*)

Perhaps there is a trace of truth, for the Capricornian likes a good sex life, but experience shows that they are not more 'given to the flesh' than other types, and are indeed remarkably constant to their beloved, even in an age when constancy has become something of a joke. The point about Capricorn is that he is an extremely stable character, constant in most things, and the image of a 'lecherous person' is certainly not fair. Equally unfair is the image of melancholy, and one vaguely wonders how a person may at once be melancholic and 'lecherous'—surely lechery is a delightful cure for the other? The image has persisted for centuries because Capricorn was accorded the rule of Saturn, who even in the second century is pretty weighty:

it will adduce among men lingering diseases consumptions, declines, rheumatisms, disorders from watery humours, and attacks of the quiet ague; as well as exile, poverty and a general mass of evils, grieves, and alarms: deaths will also be frequent, but chiefly among persons advanced in age... The atmosphere would become dreadful, chilly and frosty, unwholesome, turbulent, gloomy, presenting only clouds and pestilence. (2nd century:*4*)

It is from this that the melancholy of Capricorn is derived, for Saturn is the bent old man, the prototype of Old Father Time (figure 170). Yet the characteristics of Capricorn are no longer as black as those painted in earlier centuries, and it would seem that the power of Saturn has been broken. The following description, from the beginning of our own century, misses all reference to lechery, and mitigates the tradition of melancholy:

Self-possessed and self controlled, patient, persistent, persevering, steady, just, economical, reserved, subtle; disposition serious, cold

172

173. The horoscope of Michaelangelo,
showing the strong Capricornian
influence, with the Moon very close to
the Capricornian Ascendant.

174. Mediaeval volvelle (a device used for
casting horoscopes and for working out
Feast days. Capricorn is depicted as a
goat, though he does have a vestige of
a fish tail left.)

| 217 | 16 |

ANNO

1475

MARTIO

D. H. M.

Michael Angelus Florentinus.

2   15   37   P. M.

173

174

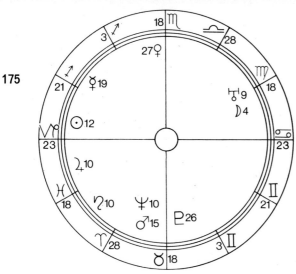

114

175

175. *The horoscope of Joseph Stalin, who was strongly Capricornian.*

176. *Three pictures of Stalin, taken from the Russian police files.*

177. *Paul Cezanne, the French painter, who was strongly Capricornian. His interest in underlying structures, and in formal composition, was typical of a Capricornian.*

176

sometimes despondent. *Fortune:* suited for public life, public appointments, business, politics; generally possess practical business ability and tact, sometimes much ambition, love of power or wealth and ability to gain it. Inheritance from parents probable. More fortunate in middle or old age than in youth. (1905:*5*)

The last sentence is particularly applicable: the Capricornian comes into himself when the age of Saturn is reached (figure 135). However our study is not of the ages of man but of a Capricornian who has been maligned and misrepresented through history because of the rulership of Saturn. A fair sample is found in a seventeenth-century textbook:

Makes a man grave, subtle, crafty, musing of great and high things, secret, solitary, painful, heapers of Riches, Niggards, studious, of their own good, full of jealousy, weak and unfortunate he giveth a depraved mind, musing of base things, quarrelsome, negligent, fearful, sad, envious, stubborn, suspicious, back biters, superstitious, rude, deceivers of such that trust them. (1651:*6*)

The dark influence of Saturn is obviously very strong and we must lighten the image immediately by saying that many Capricornians, particularly the women, are neither Niggards, back-biters, nor deceivers nor indeed miserable looking, and in fact some of them are extremely beautiful. The 'blood and thunder' image of Capricorn had, by the nineteenth century, become so unfair, so governed by Saturn, that efforts were made to represent Capricorn in a more accurate image. This meant that the black sheep of the zodiacal twelve had to be represented more like the constructive goat-fish which he was originally. The result is that one astrological description of that period presents him, quite rightly, as the 'most brilliant and the most depressed sign in the Zodiac'. Two Victorian accounts of 'the new Capricorn' will, between them, rectify the depressing image which so far has been built from earlier sources:

People born under it are deep thinkers, natural orators, and teachers. They are worshippers of intellect, and devotees to book

178. Johann Kepler, the seventeenth century German astrologer and astronomer, who was born under Capricorn. Capricornians are often interested in mathematics. He wrote of astrology: '...unfailing experience of mundane events in harmony with the changes occurring in the heavens, has compelled my unwilling belief'.

177

178

179

180

knowledge. They are insatiable in their desire for intellectual growth. They are indefatigable workers, and apt to tire quickly because they usually do several things at a time... They are not overstocked with self-esteem, and are apt to be self-conscious. Capricorn people resent all interference, and never meddle with the affairs of others. They are fine entertainers, and have excellent memories, and excel in story telling. This is the most brilliant and the most depressed sign in the Zodiac. When jolly, these Capricorners are very jolly; when miserable, they are more miserable than all the others put together, and can usually give no adequate reason for their wretchedness. They are kind-hearted, loyal, secretive. A friend once is a friend always. They are usually careful in all money and business affairs, and a promise is sacredly regarded. They are natural planners, and know how to make both ends meet. (1894:7) ...Persons who are of the type of Saturn are by nature melancholy, distrustful, cautious to timidity, yet most independent of interference or control. Intellectually speaking, they are studious, patient, curious—'inquirers'—fond of research (especially in regard to occult, and out-of-the-way-subjects), sceptical, positive, slow to think and disposed to argue—they are abstemious, economical, often 'close-fisted', but very *conscientious*, fond of solitude and indifferent to marriage—being often absolutely disposed to dislike the opposite sex; at the same time they are somewhat jealous and very constant where they once place their affections. They never act in a hurry, are grave, sober, rather suspicious and apprehensive

181

179. *Sagittarius, in the modern idiom, has been extended to cover space flight.*
180. *Capricorn governs Oxford.*
181. *Sagittarius, from a mediaeval treatise.*
182. *'At the Moulin Rouge' by the Sagittarian painter Toulouse-Lautrec. The vitality and exuberant colouring of Lautrec's paintings, as well as the unconventionality of the compositions, make him a typical Sagittarian painter.*

182

183

of consequences, and never let other people know too much on account of too great loquacity. They are fond of music and mathematics; are bigoted in their opinions, and seldom particular about their personal appearance. (1899:*8*)

More flattering, perhaps, than the traditional descriptions, but certainly more accurate: loyal, studious, intellectual, conscientious and reliable—what more can one require of a human being? The goat is a long way away, as is the old man with his sickle. With the personalized descriptions given by Alan Leo we arrive at the Capricornian zenith—reminding us that our sign rules the tenth house, the highest point in the horoscope figure— for it emphasises the steadiness, the reliability of our type, as well as the innate sensitivity:

SUN IN CAPRICORN. The 'vital principle' of the Sun's ray industrious, and persevering character, possessing independence, self-reliance, determination, thrift, and prudence, with the ability to acquire wealth and possessions. Your character will tend to become more patient, enduring and economical: you will respect age and ancient customs, possess a strong individuality, and have a love of the mystical. This sign will increase your ideality, and give you a love of beauty. It will also give you a love of justice, chastity and perfection, and you will surely succeed through your sterling traits of character. This sign gives you the ability and power to undertake responsibilities, and also tends to steady the whole character, and make it trustworthy and reliable. (1904:*9*)

This is Saturn exalted, shorn of his earlier gloom. Capricorn is restored to his position as the reliable element in society, the 'Priest or Ambassador'* as one astrologer called him. Capricorn may often appear rather dominating to those who do not like being controlled, but *someone* has to shoulder life's responsibilities. Just as Saturn rules the human skeleton (figure 185), the power enabling cosmic man to stand upright, so the Capricornian gives structure to the human world—he is the force which prevents us all from being lost in mere anarchy, the great stabilizer in the world of man.

184

* *From Pioneer to Poet.* Isabelle M. Pagan. 1911.

183. *A rather florid rendering of austere Capricorn, from a mediaeval book on astrology. (British Museum).*

184. *Pasteur, the Capricornian chemist, in his laboratory. Just as a Capricornian is interested in the larger structures of the universe, he is also interested in the minute structures, which is why he is often involved with chemistry.*

185. *Capricorn has rule over the skeleton, that which gives structure and form to the body. This skeleton is from a book by the Capricornian Culpeper.*

186. *Uranus, the ruler of Aquarius, being castrated by Saturn. Uranus governs disruptive events.*

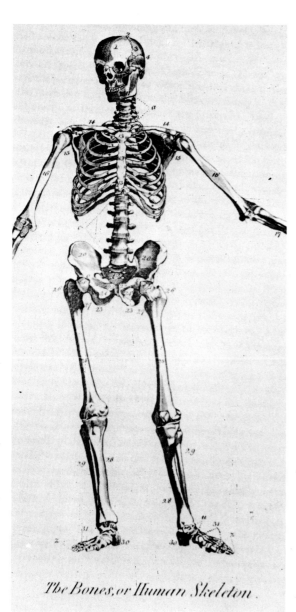

The Bones, or Human Skeleton.

185

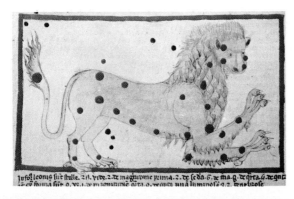

187

188

187. *Leo from a mediaeval manuscript.
(British Museum).*

188. *'The Fall of an Avalanche in the
Grisons', by the Capricornian painter
Turner. (Tate Gallery). The subject,
the mountains and the rocks are all
ruled by this sign.*

189. *'La chanteuse de Serpentes' by the
Aquarian painter Henri Rousseau.
The strange forboding atmosphere,
the strangeness of imagery and the
weird colouring, make this a typical
Aquarian painting.*

189

190. *Aquarius the Water Bearer, in the fixed stars. (From Bevis).*

191. *Aquarius the scientist, perhaps rather bedevilled by the products of his own mind: the main danger which threatens all Aquarians.*

192. *Saturn, the old ruler of Aquarius. Although Aquarians do sometimes manifest Saturnian traits, they are more obviously governed by the rebellious Uranus.*

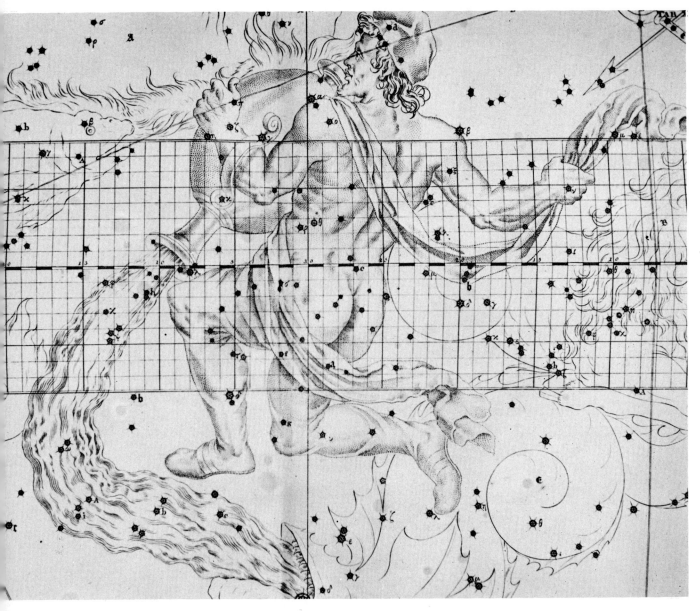

190

AQUARIUS

Aquarius, Intimates a very human affable party, speaking soberly, envious to none; constant to his opinion. (1671:*1*)

This seventeenth-century quotation is rather restrained, and in no way describes the kind of Aquarian we would recognise today—that artistic, lively, revolutionary, free-thinking individual who is supposed to represent the Age* which is to come (figure 217). We may understand why this quotation seems to be out of place nowadays when we consider that until the nineteenth century Aquarius was ruled by the planet Saturn, whose workings we saw darkly manifest in Capricorn. This is why Saturn sits in a chariot with Capricorn on one wheel and Aquarius on the other (figure 192). Such a ruler could only limit a personality, making him sober and constant, and induce the very qualities the modern Aquarian is not supposed to have. By the end of the nineteenth century, however, the image of the Aquarian disposition had changed:

191

> Sun in Aquarius gives a middle stature: a corpulent body; of fair proportions; round, full face: light brown hair; clear complexion; good disposition, though tinctured with pride and ambition; artistic or scientific. (1879:*2*)

The 'affable party' who speaks soberly has become proud and ambitious, 'artistic or scientific'. The change is due to the influence of Uranus, that planet which is at once destructive and the bringer of genius. While it is agreed by almost all astrologers that Aquarius loves above all things personal freedom, it is suggested that there are in fact two rather distinct types, and that broadly speaking one is of the artistic type, the other of the scientific type, the

192

* *Few astrologers agree on whether or not the 'Age of Aquarius' has yet begun, or is just about to begin. The present author considers it unlikely to begin until well into the next century.*

124

193

194

division corresponding to the dual rule of Saturn and Uranus. One is indeed quiet and restrained; the other noisy, and somewhat showy:

...it [Aquarius] produces several rather distinct types. The purely saturnine Aquarian resembles a Capricornian in his seriousness and his grave outlook on life, but he is as a rule far less practical; the mind is much more idealistic, and may spend much time in abstract thoughts and dreams, often on problems of philosophy, and religion, and sociology, and the result may be a lack of practical common sense. On the other hand, there is nearly always much kindness, sympathy, and refinement, together with an intense love for the feeling of kinship with wild nature. There is generally artistic ability. The love of friends is very marked, and the native—in a contradistinction to the strongly individual opposed sign, Leo—is attracted to societies, clubs, associations, groups of people, and 'movements' of all sorts, easily merging his own personality in 'causes'. (1925:3)

The first of these Aquarian types, the scientific, is obviously linked with the grave Saturn; the second with the new Uranus. Accordingly, to understand the modern image of the Aquarian we have to look mainly at nineteenth- and twentieth-century sources, for prior to this time all the descriptions related entirely and specifically to the Saturnian Aquarian. Before the prevalent image of Aquarius was developed, there had been an attempt among astrologers to link together the two planets so that the serious side of Saturn and the rebellious, creative side of Uranus were yoked together in a rather unlikely union:

The people born under Aquarius are the most perfect in form, next to those born under Libra... They are usually short, of a sanguine and fair complexion, with hazle eyes; exquisite in form, graceful in carriage. It is one of the most beautiful and esoteric signs. If you can imagine a perfect mind in a perfect body, you can get some idea of what an Aquarius person should be... Aquarian people are almost unconventional, unorthodox, breaking up formulae. In character they are refined,

steady, quiet, plodding, and unobtrusive. They express all the qualities of Saturn, but while Saturn belongs to the lower mind or *manas*, these are 'breaking through the lower mind and talking through the higher'. They are the water bearers pouring out the waters of the world. They are concentrated and clear in projecting their thoughts, concise and logical. Being good reasoners, they are also good teachers. Aquarius is the head and centre of the serving trinity; so these people are always trying to serve their fellow creatures, but they do not let people know that they are serving them by telling them about it. They are lovers of freedom and liberty, whole-souled, aspirational, and prophetic; they are also good healers...A main feature of those born under this sign is the power of imagination, stronger here than in any other sign. They are clever at picture forming, so they make good artists and painters of word pictures. Their inventive power and imagination are of the highest type. This power of concentrative thought and imagination makes them often quickly gifted with clairvoyance; more especially if they have their sun in Aquarius. They have a great power over people who are mentally afflicted, and are able to soothe them in a remarkable manner. If you talk with an Aquarian and try to draw him out, you will get hold of ideas quicker and clearer than with other people. He is persevering, quietly and steadily going on step by step – never a fuss – not looking for results but working from the pure love of service... Aquarius people are vigorous reformers, either of persons or conditions, or of the world generally. And they have the peculiar characteristic of always standing up for the unpopular beliefs...These people have little or no physical magnetism; but they magnetise mentally and they have a great power of fascination, whereby, if regulated they work a lot of mischief in the opposite sex...

When a person born under Aquarius is undeveloped he is subtle, cunning, and artful to a degree, and most clever in mental deceptions. Such types however, are rare. (1899:4)
Far removed as this quotation is from the

197

197. *The horoscope for the United States, showing an Aquarian Ascendant with Moon in this sign. Traditionally the USA is governed by Cancer, however. The heralding angel below holds an*
197. *eighteenth century version of this.*
198. *Baden-Powell, an Aquarian youth leader.*
199. *The horoscope of Abraham Lincoln.*
200. *Portrait of Abraham Lincoln, who looks very Aquarian.*

198

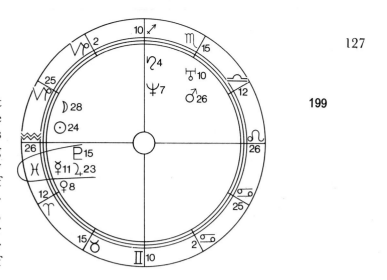

199

seventeenth century, we are still not arriving at an image of the 'free' Aquarian of today. There is still too much emphasis on Saturn, almost as if the Aquarian is the heavy god himself, living in a beautiful form – an unlikely event to say the least. The earliest of the descriptions of Aquarius with which we do not feel uncomfortable, in which we recognise the modern image, is that provided by Isabelle Pagan in her section on the 'sign of the Truth Seeker or Scientist', yet even here it is the influence of Saturn which predominates:

the chief characteristic of the typical Aquarian at the highly evolved stage is, as is already been said, his extraordinary breadth of vision. He is absolutely unbiased and open-minded, without taint of prejudice or superstition of any kind. Tradition and authority leave him untouched. When he finds himself face to face with them, he regards them with tranquility and serenity, and possibly with a certain friendliness and interest; but no amount of natural courtesy towards them will make him veil his sight or refrain from turning on them the search-light of the truth seeker. His ways are neither militant nor aggressive. He can wait; and the longer he waits, the more clearly he realises the difficulty of attaining certainty about anything that is worth knowing, and the folly of condemning too hastily the theories of other truth seekers, who are just as likely to be in the right as he is. This results in an entire lack of pose, and perfect freedom from vanity and self-conceit as far as knowledge is concerned. He is willing to learn from anyone, even from a little child. If after patient enquiry and deep probing he realises that he has made a discovery or exposed a fallacy, he is generally eager to pass the information on to others as quickly as possible, even if in so doing he has to recant views he has formerly advocated, and abandon some of his favourite theories. He is, in fact, the finest possible type of scientist; not necessarily the practical scientist who utilises universal law on the physical plane, but simply the student of these laws, the truth seeker, patient, dispassionate and untiring, whose method is to take a comprehensive

200

201

201. 'Young girl Bathing' by the French
painter Renoir. The painting, like
all the paintings of Renoir, is more
Piscean than Aquarian. (National
Museum, Oslo).
202. The horoscope of Renoir.
203. A Piscean scene by a Capricornian
artist. Venice is governed by Pisces,
whilst Turner was Capricornian. The
water points to Pisces, the subdued
colours and the structure to Capricorn.

202

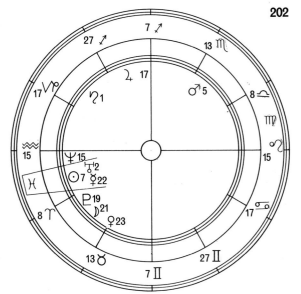

203

view of his subject, form his own hypothesis, and then marshal his facts, trying and testing his theories until they are proof against assault. In fact 'What is the *truth* of the matter?' is his one concern, and the pet question of the prosaic craftsman – who often advances a bogus claim to a scientific attitude of mind – 'What is the *use* of it?' rarely enters into his calculations at all. (1911:5)

The impression one gets from the passage is that the Aquarian is still trying to free himself from the restrictive influence of Saturn – he is looking for an identity. Talk of the brotherhood of man, the use of words which pass on a superficial level for love, the brash self-assertion associated with the youthful Aquarian, all this is a disguise for a type who is looking for himself, seeking a working inner structure which will relate harmoniously with the outer world! Perhaps this is why the most common faults of the Aquarian is that of inefficiency, because he is not related harmoniously to himself, A more modern description of Aquarius emphasises the creativity normally associated with Uranus, the planet governing the new humanitarianism:

AQUARIUS. Artistic, idealistic, human, strong willed, frank, open, cheerful, genial, timid, scientific, interested in life rather than form, fixed and strong opinions, good judge of human nature, often break promises, ask advice, and do not follow it. (1922:6)

Aquarius is 'interested in life rather than form', which perhaps in itself goes a long way towards explaining at least two things about the Aquarian. First, why the Aquarian is so often creative; and second, why a different Aquarius appears in every age – for the one factor of which we can be certain is that history is a record of changes of attitude in life. The nature of Aquarius, whether of the quiet Saturnine type or the more disruptive Uranus, is notoriously difficult to pin down – Aquarius is of the element Air, and anyone who has tried to catch air may understand the difficulties involved. For the best modern description of Aquarius we must of necessity turn to the collection of character delineations made by Waite at the beginning of our century:

In the lower type of Aquarius the Uranian influence is even more marked, for then we see the firey and erratic temper, extreme independence, sudden fits of eccentricity and seething internal unrest, reminding one of a volcano which may erupt at any minute, perverse and threatening in its silence as it gives off the fumes of anger. These fits of strange and often unaccountable silence are a marked feature of the sign, and even in the more evolved types they will occasionally be noticed, making the Aquarian a very difficult person to understand and get on with when in these moods...

Some of their peculiarities are a desire to be quite alone at times; to resent the interference or even help of others in their work unless they are in command; to be very reserved and secretive if questioned on any matter, when if left to tell their tale at their own time they would be quite frank. They are also subject to many disappointments and disillusionments with regard to other people, for they read character so quickly that the outer veneer of society does not hold them long entranced, and they seem to feel, as a consequence, a kind of mental isolation and solitude. If they become attached to others they are very faithful and seem to be able to hold their friends and lovers in a very marked manner. At the same time, they do not readily give their confidence to other people, and it is practically impossible for them to 'make friends' again if once offended or deceived, so deep is their resentment and sensitiveness. Though their friendships are usually life-long and no sacrifice is too great for those they love, they are generally undemonstrative...

The mentality is very clear and profound, fitting them for literary and scientific pursuits. There is much originality and usually a marked gift for character impersonations, poetry, novel-writing, or music... (1917:7)

Waite's excellent account of Aquarius leaves us with no doubt that our type, when not under any great pressure, is gentle, intelligent and creative – a combination of qualities rare enough to impress anyone. Let us hope that the Age of Aquarius lives up to this promise...

204. *Pisces the Fishes, joined by a cord, in the fixed stars.*

205. *The eternal Piscean female lost in her dreams. All the watery types are great dreamers: sometimes they are able to put their dreams into some art form.*

206. *Neptune, with his strange seahorses, the modern ruler of Pisces.*

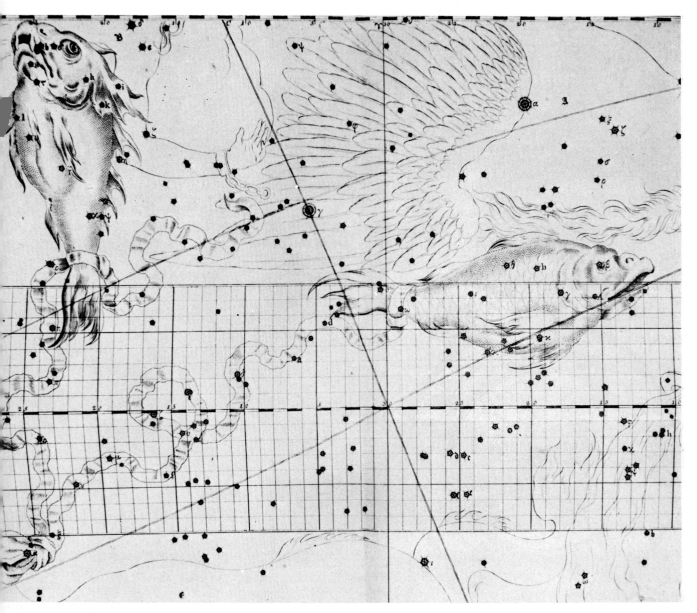

204

PISCES

Pisces gives a short ill composed body, yet a good face, something large, of a pale, yet clear complexion, thick shoulders, brown hair, fat and plump in all parts, sluggish and, slothful. (1679:*1*)

A pity to begin a description of this charming type with such words as 'sluggish and slothful', for having admitted that Pisceans do tend to be lazy, there are much nicer and more apposite things one can say. Yet the curious thing is that Pisces, for some reason or another, did have an unfortunate reputation in the past, as a further quotation will confirm:

Pisces, argues a stammering person, fraudulent, and a pretender to the Truth. (1671:*2*)

This is also from the seventeenth century. The unfortunate reputation is all the more curious when we consider that Pisces was ruled by the beneficient, expansive, and honest Jupiter – no more a stammerer than fraudulent (figure 207). With the discovery of the planet Neptune, (which astrologers, quite rightly, determined was an extremely sensitive planet – 'Neptune the mystic', it was called) the rulership over watery Pisces was transferred to its tender care, as being more suitable to a 'watery' planet, and there was an immediate change of attitude to Pisces. By the nineteenth century, astrologers' descriptions of Pisces, though they still harped on the faults of Pisces, were more gentle than earlier astrologers in their dealings:

Sun in Pisces describes a short, fleshy person; round face; good complexion; light-brown or flaxen hair; a harmless disposition, may be own enemy by reason of extravagance, and indulgence in feasting and pleasure. (1879:*3*)

Pisces the fraudulent has now become Pisces

205

206

207

208

the harmless, and very shortly he will become good-natured:

>...easy-going, good-natured, indolent, uncertain, changeful, emotional, charitable, affectionate; sometimes diffident and reserved or secretive. *Fortune*: benefit through philanthropic humanitarian movements; domesticated and home-loving; inclined to almsgiving, works of charity, religion, nursing, helping the poor or sick, and may themselves benefit in some cases. Taste for music, romantic and imaginative work, novel writing. Good and faithful servants under superiors. (1905:*4*)

To understand the type we shall have to look into the nature of its modern ruler Neptune, who was the Greek Posideon, the god of the sea, and whose trident, some astrologers say, now symbolizes the modern planet:

>The planet Neptune seems to be a typical representative of the psychic plane in Nature, and to have affinity with the watery signs of the zodiac. Water stands for the woman as opposed to the man; for the Moon-nature as opposed to the Sun-nature; for that which is receptive and responsible to stimulus from without, as contrasted with that which is positive, non-receptive, and self-motivated. The following are the keys to the nature of this planet:
>
>(1) 'Unstable as water' is a suitable description of Neptune: unstable, constantly changing, unreliable, and not to be depended on. It overthrows things, and operates in some cases even more unexpectedly than Uranus (though rarely so *suddenly*). Uranus is the Wind, blowing where it listeth; Neptune the Water, less stable even than the shifting sand, engulfing the solid earth and overthrowing the ambitious works of man.
>
>(2) The 'watery' nature, as manifested in human character, is instinctive and intuitive rather than intellectual. It is not bound by the rules of the logical faculty, and its conclusions are based, in part, upon evidence not furnished by the five senses. When prominent for good, therefore, Neptune may assist the manifestation of genius, may inspire the mind with ideas derived from inner planes of nature, and

may attract towards the spiritual. But when afflicted in an evil horoscope this planet may be the vehicle for all sorts of undesirable influences from the astral plane of Nature, temptations that appeal to the passional, emotional, and sense-loving side of the animal man; and it may incline towards a passive and injurious kind of mediumship. When well aspected in a good horoscope, however, this may take on a much higher form, resulting in normal seer-ship.

(3) A third key to the planet's influence lies in the emotional and sensational characteristics shown by those in whom the passional nature predominates. A love of luxury, of fine sensations and the things of the senses; and emotional nature easily aroused by slight stimulus: a fondness for novelty, and anything that causes a new sensation; a changeable and versatile nature, with fickle enthusiasms – these are characteristics of Neptune.

(4) Just as water passively reflects the images of things, and shapes itself to bodies with which it comes in contact, so the child of Neptune is imitative, thinks the thoughts of others, is too much influenced by the example of others and is almost as much moved by the joys and sorrows of others as if they were his own. Neptune thus provides actors of all sorts; visionary enthusiasts who create their own Madonnas, and reproduce the stigmata on their own persons; detectives, who reflect in themselves the thought of the criminal; thought readers, novelists and lawyers, who work by plot and counter-plot; imitative imaginations, who resort to opium and other drugs to produce fictitious visions and artificial exaltations of faculty; also pretenders and imposters, as well as natural actors... (1904:5) Pisces, the sign ruled by Neptune, will therefore be receptive, intuitive emotional, imitative and extremely imaginative, and indeed those words do convey very well the nature of the Piscean being. At the same time these very qualities suggest that the type will at the other extreme be unreliable, changeable, impelled by a love of sensation, and given to impulse. The contradictory characteristics are the very root of the Piscean being. Looking at the virtues and

207. *Jupiter the traditional ruler of Pisces, as the small circle at his left foot suggests. Jupiter is rarely as violent as this strange image would suggest: perhaps he is angry with Neptune for usurping his rulership over Pisces.*

208. *The world destroyed by water.*

209. *'The Admiral' by Archimboldo. An extremely Piscean rendering of a human face.*

209

the vices in a little more depth shows that these are never separated and clear-cut, as with other types, but in a constant state of flux in the one Piscean person. The main virtues have been listed in the following manner.:

These people have a deep, hidden love-nature, and are always anxious to give of their abundance to all who need. They are natural lovers, and their realm is the kingdom of the soul. They rarely look for dishonesty; on the contrary, are prone to have too much confidence in the words and promises of those they love. They are very loyal to their friends and will defend them, whether right or wrong. It is almost impossible for the average Pisces person to acknowledge a flaw in the person cared for. These are the people who will deny themselves the absolute comforts of life to further the interests of relative or friend. These are also the people of quick attractions and equally quick repulsions, though they are generally too kind to let their aversions be seen. They are very fond of beautiful things in nature and art, and among them are to be found excellent art critics, artists, and writers... Those born under this sign do not demand quite so much as they give; if they did they would be the most difficult people on earth to live with. They are naturally very honest and clean-minded, and the women are easily disgusted with anything coarse or common. In marriage they become very unhappy if the relation is degraded into a merely sexual one... There are very few egotists to be found among Pisces people. In fact, they are in many instances abnormally deficient in self-esteem, and this causes them to appear very awkward and sometimes leads to the belief that all the world is against them, and it is of no use to try to keep up in the race with others. (1894:6)

The faults spring mainly from the innate sensitivity of the type; from his being a victim of the world, in a sense – in being a sensitive soul lost in a world which has little respect for sensitivity. Many Pisceans believe that they have been born in the wrong day and age, and perhaps there is truth in this. The various gambits, by which Pisceans try to hide their sensitivity and their inability to deal with the

210. 'The Crucifixion' by Raphael. The two thousand years subsequent to the birth of Christ, have, according to tradition, been governed by Pisces.

211. Pisces the Fishes, from a mediaeval manuscript. (British Museum).

212. The nativity of a gentlewoman 'extremely subject to scandals and imprisonments'. The twelfth house, governed by Pisces, is sometimes called the 'house of one's own undoing'.

213. Ellen Terry the actress. She is Piscean by birth and appearance.

214. Mr. Micawber, the famous Dickensian character, who has been described by some astrologers as the perfect male Piscean, because he is always lost in dreams and hopeful speculations which bear little relationships to reality. Pisceans are often waiting for something to 'turn up', just like Mr. Micawber.

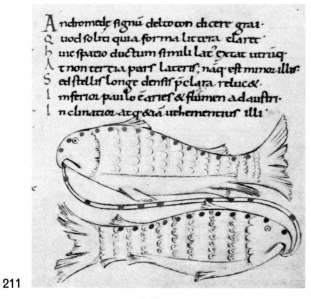

211

212

213

214

136

215

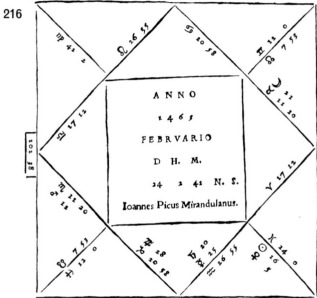

216

217

215. *The horoscope of Mary Queen of Scots, who had Sun and Mercury in Pisces.*

216. *The horoscope of the great humanist Pico della Mirandola, who had both the Sun and Venus in Pisces. Pisceans are often great mystics, and are always highly sensitive.*

217. *Venice, the city of Pisces, seen through the eyes of a Libran painter, Canaletto.*

world, at times include deceit, hypocrisy, and lying – three faults which emerge from a lack of real self-confidence. Many Pisceans turn to liquor in order to escape their condition. The extremes are rarely met with, (the suicidal tendencies associated with the twelfth house, the traditional 'House of One's Own Undoing', being less common than many astrologers would have us believe) and the following account of Piscean faults is fairly well-balanced: Some of these people beat their hearts out with imagining fears, and are constantly expecting accidents and unpleasant tidings... The women are wavering and uncertain in all their actions, They lose their belongings and mislay those of other people. They drop things and forget to pick them up, and sometimes are so superlatively careless in all household matters that even their sweet and helpful dispositions cannot make up for the trouble they can create in a well-ordered household. These are the people who kick up mats and rugs, and never seem aware that they do not leave things exactly as they found them. There is a peculiar obstinacy in the Pisces character, which sometimes becomes a most formidable element to deal with, and really seems inexplicable, but it is easily explained. The natural timidity and abnormal delicacy of these people acts as a constant restraint, and after a while the nature becomes tired of the yoke of its own placing and revels.

At this crisis they show a stubborness which is even more disagreeable than that of the stiff-necked Taurus, and they have neither logic nor consistency.

They will say and do the most absurd things,

218. The Aquarian age to come opens mankind to two possibilities: he may develop the Uranian side of his nature, and learn self-control, and love for the humanity of which we are all significant fragments, and thus fly skywards as his proper nature demands; or he may rebel against the natural world which surrounds him, allow his inventions to invite his own destruction.

and stick to them. At such times, argument and advice are useless. The more they are reasoned with, the more obstinate they become. In the acceptance of a new theory or truth which they have previously repudiated, the males are quite likely to declare that it is precisely what they have always believed. One of the great faults of this sign is intellectual dishonesty.

Pisces people are apt to talk too much, and they have a tedious habit of asking questions. When united in marriage to those who object to giving an account of themselves, and who, as in the case of Libra people, have no patience with those who exact reasons and explanations, serious trouble is the inevitable result...

218

Their faults can be summed up in restlessness, recklessness, recklessness in giving, lack of judgement and discrimination, and disloyalty to self. These people are the ones who efface themselves for others, to the detriment of those they assist, and their own health and prosperity. They are careless with their words, very illogical, constantly asking questions, and never waiting for answers. (1894:7)

The faults are scarcely *serious* ones, then, for they spring more from a general inability to take the ordinary world seriously than from any inherent criminality. There is a delightful fairy-like quality about some Pisceans, which those devoted to the world so glibly called 'real' find rather repellent. If fairyland had a ruling sign, it would surely be Pisces, and this in itself a sufficient advertisement that the Piscean is possessed of more virtues than vices, no matter how ethereal these virtues might be!

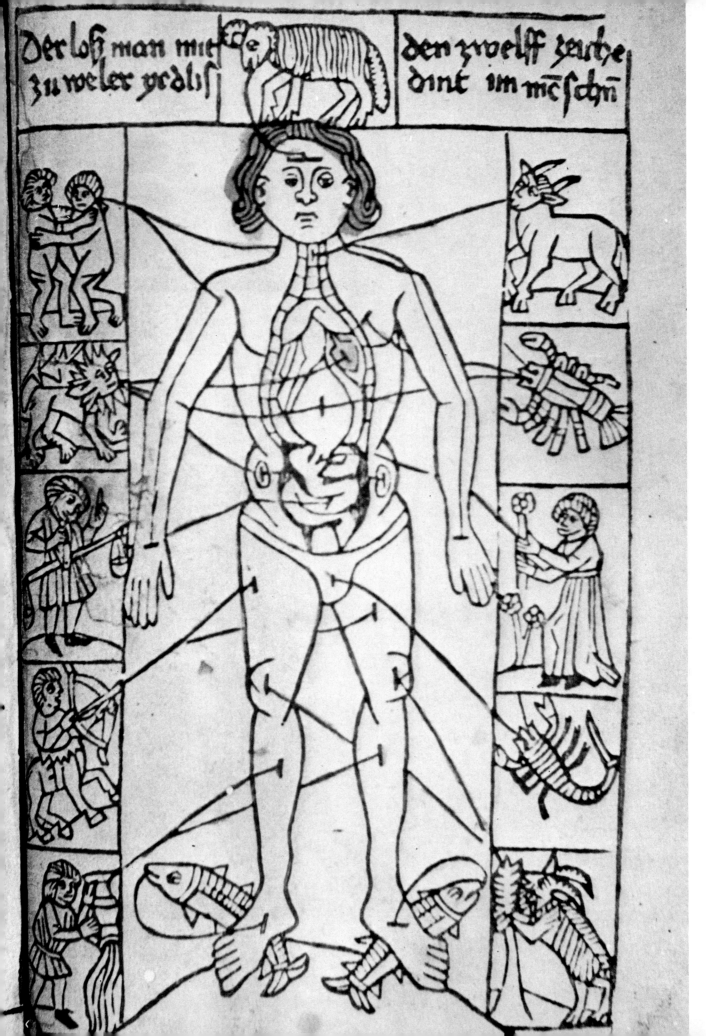

BIBLIOGRAPHY

I would like to thank those of my friends and students who have helped me with constructive criticism and artwork whilst the foregoing book was in preparation: Maureen Clarke, John Hardy, Clare Johns, Joan Lacy, Angela Macdonald, Jane Paterson, Robert Powell, Anne Roberts, Andrew Tweedie and my wife. In particular, I would like to thank Elizabeth Inwood for her delightful drawings of the twelve types, and Julia Franco for help with the paste-up of proofs. My thanks and good wishes to my teachers.

Bibliographic references in the twelve chapters on the signs:

Bevis John	*The Celestial Atlas* 1789	
Bewick Thomas	*History of Quadrupeds* 1790 *History of British Birds* 1797	
Fludd Robert	*Utriusque Cosmi Historia* 1626	
Lilly William	*Monarchy or No Monarchy* 1651 *Christian Astrology* 1647	
Sibly Ebenezer	*A New and Complete Illustration of the Occult Sciences* 1795	
Pagan Isabelle	*From Pioneer to Poet* 1911	
Porté De la	*Physiognomie* 1623	
Varley John	*Treatise on Zodiacal Physiognomy* 1828	

Bibliographic references in the Introduction:

(1679:*1*)   John Gadbury
Quoted by John Partridge in
An Astrological Vade Mecum

(1679:*2*)   John Gadbury
(*supra*)

(1671:*3*)   William Thrasher
Jubar Astrologicum, or a True Astrological Guide

(2nd Century A.D. – 4)
Ptolemy
Quoted by John Partridge *An Astrological Vade Mecum*

ARIES

(1879:*1*)   Alfred John Pearce
The Textbook of Astrology

(1795:*2*)   Ebenezer Sibly
A New and Complete Illustration of the Occult Sciences

(1795:*3*)   Ebenezer Sibly (*supra*)

(1795:*4*)   Ebenezer Sibly (*supra*)

(1795:*5*)   Ebenezer Sibly (*supra*)

(1911:*6*) Isabelle M. Pagan
From Pioneer to Poet

(1679:*7*) John Partridge
An Astrological Vade Mecum

(1917:*8*) Herbert T. Waite
Compendium of Natal Astrology
(With the permission of the
publishers, Kegan Paul and Co.)

(1893:*9*) 'Sephariel'
(Walter Gorn Old)
The Astrologer's Magazine No. 34

(1904:*10*) 'Leo' (William Allan)
The Art of Synthesis

(1904:*11*) 'Leo' (William Allan)
(*supra*)

TAURUS

(1795:*1*) Ebenezer Sibly
*A New and Complete Illustration of the
Occult Sciences*

(1647:*2*) William Lilly
Christian Astrology

(1911:*3*) Isabelle M. Pagan
From Pioneer to Poet.
(With the permission of the
Publishers: The Theosophical
Publishing House)

(1795:*4*) Ebenezer Sibly
(*supra*)

(c. 2nd Century A.D. – 5)
Ptolemy
Tetrabiblos. (Ashmand Translation
of 1822).

(1795:*6*) Ebenezer Sibly
(*supra*)

(1911:*7*) Isabelle M. Pagan
(*supra*)

(1904:*8*) 'Leo' (William Allan)
The Art of Synthesis

(1928:*9*) Charles E. O. Carter.
The Zodiac and the Soul.
(With the permission of the
Publishers: The Theosophical
Publishing House).

GEMINI

(1879:*1*) Alfred John Pearce
The Textbook of Astrology

(1911:*2*) Isabelle M. Pagan
From Pioneer to Poet

(1911:*3*) Isabelle M. Pagan (*supra*)

(1647:*4*) William Lilly
Christian Astrology

(1647:*5*) William Lilly (*supra*)

(1647:*6*) William Lilly (*supra*)

(1647:*7*) William Lilly (*supra*)

(1922:*8*) Vivian E. Robson
A Student's Text-Book of Astrology.
(With the permission of the
Publishers: Cecil Palmer).

(1925:*9*) Charles E. O. Carter.
The Principles of Astrology. (With the
permission of the Publishers: The
Theosophical Publishing House).

(1828:*10*) John Varley
Treatise on Zodiacal Physiognomy

(1679:*11*) John Partridge
An Astrological Vade Mecum

(1910:*12*) 'Leo' (William F. Allan)
The Key to your own Nativity

(1911:*13*) Isabelle M. Pagan
(*supra*)

(1894:*14*) Eleanor Kirk
*The Influence of the Zodiac Upon
Human Life.*

(1905:*1*) 'Leo' (William F. Allan)
Complete Dictionary of Astrology

(1647:*2*) William Lilly
Christian Astrology

(1647:*3*) William Lilly
(*supra*)

(1795:*4*) Ebenezer Sibly
*A New and Complete Illustration of the
Occult Sciences*

(1890:*5*) W. J. Simmonite
*The Arcana of Practical Astral
Philosophy*

(1910:*6*) 'Leo' (William F. Allan)
The Key to Your Own Nativity

(1911:*7*) Isabelle M. Pagan
From Pioneer to Poet. (With the permission of the Publishers: The Theosophical Publishing House).

(1894:*8*) Eleanor Kirk
The Influence of the Zodiac Upon Human Life.

LEO

(1879:*1*) Alfred John Pearce
The Textbook of Astrology

(1795:*2*) Ebenezer Sibly
A New and Complete Illustration of the Occult Sciences

(1894:*3*) Eleanor Kirk
The Influence of the Zodiac Upon Human Life

(1917:*4*) Herbert T. Waite.
Compendium of Natal Astrology. (With the permission of the Publishers: Kegan Paul and Co.)

(1917:*5*) Herbert T. Waite *(supra)*

(1679:*6*) John Partridge
An Astrological Vade Mecum

(1894:*7*) Eleanor Kirk *(supra)*

(1910:*8*) 'Leo' (William F. Allan)
The Key to Your Own Nativity

(1910:*9*) 'Leo' (William F. Allan) *(supra)*

(1894:*10*) Eleanor Kirk *(supra)*

(1911:*11*) Isabelle M. Pagan
From Pioneer to Poet. (With the permission of the Publishers: The Theosophical Publishing House).

VIRGO

(1679:*1*) John Partridge
An Astrological Vade Mecum

(1647:*2*) William Lilly
Christian Astrology

(1879:*3*) Alfred John Pearce
The Textbook of Astrology

(1647:*4*) William Lilly
(supra)

(1925:*5*) Charles E. O. Carter.
The Principles of Astrology (With the permission of the Publishers: The Theosophical Publishing House).

(1964:*6*) R. P. Lister
Astrology – The Astrologers' Quarterly – vol. 38. No. 2. p.54
The Fault is in Our Stars
(Reprinted by permission of Punch).

(1897:*7*) Eleanor Kirk
The Influence of the Zodiac Upon Human Life

(1917:*8*) Herbert T. Waite
Compendium of Natal Astrology (With the permission of the Publishers: Kegan Paul and Co.)

(1911:*9*) Isabelle M. Pagan
From Pioneer to Poet. (With the permission of the Publishers: The Theosophical Publishing House)

(1905:*10*) 'Leo' (William F. Allan)
Complete Dictionary of Astrology

(1931:*11*) A. E. Thierens
Elements of Esoteric Astrology. (With the permission of the Publishers: Rider and Co.).

LIBRA

(1795:*1*) Ebenezer Sibly
A New and Complete Illustration of the Occult Sciences

(1894:*2*) Eleanor Kirk
The Influence of the Zodiac Upon Human Life

(1647:*3*) William Lilly
Christian Astrology

(1795:*4*) Ebenezer Sibly
(supra)

(1905:*5*) 'Leo' (William F. Allan)
Complete Dictionary of Astrology

(1917:*6*) Herbert T. Waite
Compendium of Natal Astrology (With the permission of the Publishers: Kegan Paul and Co.)

(1847:*7*) Eleanor Kirk
(*supra*)

(1795:*8*) Ebenezer Sibly
(*supra*)

(1905:*9*) 'Leo' (William F. Allan) (*supra*)

SCORPIO

(1795:*1*) Ebenezer Sibly
A New and Complete Illustration of the Occult Sciences

(1671:*2*) William Trasher
Jubar Astrologicum or a True Astrological Guide

(1828:*3*) John Varley
Treatise on Zodiacal Physiognomy

(1675:*4*) John Gadbury
Obsequium Rationabile

(1675:*5*) John Gadbury
(*supra*)

(1899:*6*) Richard D. Stocker
Astrological Physiognomy from *The Modern Astrologer p.159*

(1910:*7*) 'Leo' (William F. Allan)
The Key to Your Own Nativity

(1894:*8*) Eleanor Kirk
The Influence of the Zodiac on Human Life

(1894:*9*) Eleanor Kirk (*supra*)

SAGITTARIUS

(1795:*1*) Ebenezer Sibly
A New and Complete Illustration of the Occult Sciences

(1651:*2*) William Lilly
Christian Astrology

(1922:*3*) Vivian E. Robson
A Student's Textbook of Astrology. (With the permission of the Publishers: Cecil Palmer)

(1651:*4*) William Lilly
(*supra*)

(1651:*5*) William Lilly
(*supra*)

(1894:*6*) Eleanor Kirk
The Influence of the Zodiac Upon Human Life

(1894:*7*) Eleanor Kirk
(*supra*)

(1893:*8*) 'Sepharial'
(Walter Gorn Old)
The Astrologers' Magazine No. 34

(1905:*9*) 'Leo' (William F. Allan)
Complete Dictionary of Astrology

CAPRICORN

(1795:*1*) Ebenezer Sibly
A New and Complete Illustration of the Occult Sciences

(1879:*2*) Alfred John Pearce
The Textbook of Astrology

(1671:*3*) William Thrasher
Jubar Astrologicum or a True Astrological Guide

(2nd Century – 4)
Ptolemy
Tetrabiblios (Ashmand translation of 1822)

(1905:*5*) 'Leo' (William F. Allan)
Complete Dictionary of Astrology

(1651:*6*) William Lilly
Christian Astrology

(1894:*7*) Eleanor Kirk
The Influence of the Zodiac Upon Human Life

(1899:*8*) Richard D. Stocker
Astrological Physiognomy from *The Modern Astrologer p. 161/2*

(1904:*9*) 'Leo' (William F. Allan)
Key to Your Own Nativity

AQUARIUS

(1671:*1*) William Thrasher
Jubar Astrologicum or a True Astrological Guide
(1879:*2*) Alfred John Pearce
The Textbook of Astrology
(1925:*3*) Charles E. O. Carter
The Principles of Astrology.
(With the permission of the Publishers: The Theosophical Publishing House)
(1899:*4*) Bessie Leo
Journal of the Astrological Society February 1899. From the transactions of the Astrological Society, December 2nd, 1898
(1911:*5*) Isabelle M. Pagan
From Pioneer to Poet. (With the permission of the Publishers: Theosophical Publishing House)
(1922:*6*) Vivian F. Robson
A Student's Textbook of Astrology. (With the permission of the Publishers: Cecil Palmer)
(1917:*7*) Herbert T. Waite
Compendium of Natal Astrology

PISCES

(1679:*1*) John Partridge
An Astrological Vade Mecum
(1671:*2*) William Trasher
Jubar Astrologicum or a True Astrological Guide
(1879:*3*) Alfred John Pearce
The Textbook of Astrology
(1905:*4*) 'Leo' (William F. Allan)
Complete Dictionary of Astrology
(1904:*5*) 'Leo' (William F. Allan)
The Art of Synthesis

(1894:*6*) Eleanor Kirk
The Influence of the Zodiac on Human Life
(1894:*7*) Eleanor Kirk
(*supra*)

Acknowledgements

The use of photographs and prints from the following collections, agencies, galleries, photographers and artists, is gratefully acknowledged:

Austrian Tourist Board: 122, 195., Mrs. Herbert Bier: 25., British Museum: 1, 2, 5, 7, 9, 10, 13, 17, 26, 33, 39, 45, 54, 61, 64, 66, 67, 69, 70, 74, 87, 101, 102, 108, 113, 114, 115, 119, 136, 140, 144, 145, 155, 159, 160, 167, 168, 187, 174, 181, 190, 203, 204, 211, 212., British Tourist Authority: 83, 138, 180., Photographie Bulloz: 137., A. C. Cooper: 106, 196., Courtauld Institute: 27., Cyprus Tourist Board: 32., Dresden: 46., Mary Evans Picture Library: 59, 186., French Tourist Office: 63, 118., Giraudon: 116, 182, 209., Michael Holford: 125, 139, 201., Hulton Picture Library: 21, 22, 23, 51, 58, 60, 62, 65, 76, 77, 78, 79, 80, 84, 94, 97, 109, 127, 148, 152, 162, 164, 176, 177, 178, 184, 193, 194, 198, 206, 208, 217., Elizabeth Inwood: 15, 40, 56, 72, 88, 104, 120, 141, 157, 169, 191, 205., Italian Tourist Office: 31, 172., Louvre: 38., Mansell Collection: 81, 82, 96, 112, 126, 128, 143, 165, 151, 171, 214., Henry P. McIlhenny: 182., Munich: Kunsthistorisches Museum: 137., Musée d'Art Modern, Paris: 68., National Army Museum: 20., National Film Archive: 218 (upper)., National Gallery, London: 90., National Gallery, Oslo: 201., Prado, Madrid: 19., Ann Roberts: 48, 107., Tate Gallery, London: 188., Andrew Tweedie: 131, 132, 133, 134, 135., Uffizi, Florence: 37, 75., United States Information Service: 149, 179, 200, 218 (lower).